七言长诗 | 汉英对照

追梦

蔡远方 著

当代世界出版社
THE CONTEMPORARY WORLD PRESS

Seven-Character Epic
in Chinese and English

To Seek
the Chinese Dream

Cai Yuanfang

图书在版编目（CIP）数据

追梦 / 蔡远方著. -- 北京：当代世界出版社，
2019.10
ISBN 978-7-5090-1522-3

Ⅰ. ①追… Ⅱ. ①蔡… Ⅲ. ①诗集—中国—当代
Ⅳ. ①I227

中国版本图书馆 CIP 数据核字 (2019) 第 221115号

书　　名：	追梦
出版发行：	当代世界出版社
地　　址：	北京市东城区地安门东大街70-9号
网　　址：	http://www.worldpress.org.cn
编务电话：	(010) 83907528
发行电话：	(010) 83908410（传真）
	13601274970
	18611107149
	13521909533
经　　销：	新华书店
印　　刷：	北京汇林印务有限公司
开　　本：	710毫米×1000毫米　1/16
印　　张：	18.25
字　　数：	160千字
版　　次：	2020年4月第1版
印　　次：	2020年4月第1次
书　　号：	ISBN 978-7-5090-1522-3
定　　价：	99.00元

如发现印装质量问题，请与承印厂联系调换。
版权所有，翻印必究；未经许可，不得转载！

推荐序

愚公"造山"

二月河

黄河之滨的王屋山,是愚公的故乡,也是他移山的地方。而今,出生在黄河之滨邙山脚下的蔡远方君,亦堪称是一位"愚公"。此君的业绩,不是移山,而是造山。他用诗词艺术,用富有知识内涵、诗情画意的七言韵语,独自创作了一部数千行的七言史诗《追梦》。诗中除了他富有才气的诗词创作,他还化用了古今中外数百位思想家、科学家、文化大家的哲学思辨、诗词精魂,描述了中国近百年的发展历程,亦展示了百余年间中华大地上的惊涛骇浪,描写了诸多影响中国现代史、当代史的代表人物,恰似一座用诗词艺术筑起的山峰。凭借数十年诗词功底,依仗胸中"中国梦"为图腾,经年累月,终集大成。远方君可称得"诗词愚公"。

诗词作品的鉴别标准不只是字数的多少,更重要的是品位和内容。《追梦》的品位,其制高点在于它不同凡响的综合品质:它不是中国现代史、当代史,却彰显着中华人民共和国七十年来志士仁人的伟大与坚韧;它不是中国志,却凝聚着深厚的中华文化历史积淀，凸显了华夏文化的厚重与传承；它不是音乐，却回荡着歌声的激情和韵律，向天国传颂着中华儿女的愿望与心声；它不是语言学、历史学课本，却包容着许许多多的历史知识、历史人物、历史事件。诸多元素的整合，在远方君的功力和才气的激荡回肠中，形成了一部具有史学深沉、哲学思辨、政治敏锐、艺术灵性的著作，且具有强劲的震撼力与吸引力，使读者内心发出对祖国、对人民、对共产党、对中国特色社会主义的景仰心与自豪感。

远方君精读了老子和孔子，精读了屈原、白居易、苏东坡，精读了毛泽东与邓小平，精读了马克思与恩格斯，精读了苏格拉底与霍金，更精读了《习近平用典》。他将诸圣诸君的思想与艺术，精心梳理，化为神器，撞出灵性，使伟大的祖国在诗歌声中肋生双翅，翱翔天空，追梦筑梦；这亦是一部具有艺术韵律的中国现代史、当代史，浓绘着中华百年，沧桑巨变，巨龙腾飞。

长卷数千行，七言韵语，中东大韵，一辙到底。或一联一咏，或绝句一题。诗词内容如歌如吟，万卉千花。又将笔锋触涉到祖国风貌的方方面面：咏人，则张扬其德行才干、变革思想、事功成就；咏事，则描绘巨龙图变、蜕壳变蛾、节节发展。更把目光投向今天和明天，将祖国改革开放以来的方方成果、种种成就融入笔墨，熠熠生辉；把明天的美好，将习近平主席设计的蓝图，彩色生成，艺术描绘。今明互映，天人一体；观书读诗，令人振奋。

待到二〇五〇时，九州犹如七彩虹；
百花吐艳争芬芳，光照寰宇气色清；
那时华夏巍然立，享誉世界唤大同；
天耀中华真善美，山花烂漫笑丛中。

这是远方君在《筑梦篇》的部分诗章，简洁嘹亮，文采激扬；将21世纪中期的中国，点睛画龙，力透纸背，诗唱并重，亦赋亦咏，可谓绝唱。

"物华天宝""人杰地灵"这样的词语，通常是对中华大地上神奇之举的溢美之词，但仅仅是一种宽泛的文学形容。远方君却用一种创造性思维，穷毕生思考，集多年时历，纵凝百年，横贯九州，以人为焦点，精灵汇华夏，把散落而精光四射的粒粒珍珠汇成一幅光照长河的美丽图画，为"物华天宝""人杰地灵"的宽泛溢美以新的聚合，为精灵充盈的东方巨龙充实了哲思、奋斗、图变、图强的丰富内含，插上了腾飞的翅膀。

赠君一碗高粱酒，以壮胆色青纱行；
敢登宇宙太空游，九州儿女志成城；
敢把长江当匹练，奔涛骇浪任驰骋；
敢持黄河长空舞，信手舒卷抒东风；
敢叫日月供调遣，风叱云咤履群峰；
敢以身为天下先，一路高歌神州行。

这些《敢当篇》中的文字，也只有喝着黄河水长大的"愚公"才能造得出来。昔日曹雪芹抱病于西山小屋，书就不世之作；今日"愚公"蜗居于樱桃园"独书斋"，耐得孤独与寂寞，两耳不闻喧闹，一心彩绘中华。

华夏厚土，山高水长；民族复兴，指日可望；文化复兴，中华不亡。神凝长天五色展，中华沃土育"愚公"。

是为《追梦》序。

2017 年 12 月

Preface

New Genesis by an Iron-Willed Man

Er Yuehe

Wangwu Mountain, which stands by the Yellow River, is the hometown of Yu Gong (literally a stupid man, and metaphorically an iron-willed man), who moved a mountain away according to Chinese myth. And now, Mr. Cai Yuanfang, who was born at the foot of Mangshan Mountain by the Yellow River, is known as Yu Gong, too. Mr. Cai's achievement lies not in moving a natural mountain, but in creating an artistic one, in that he, with his poetic art, has created a thousand-lined and seven-character poem titled *To Seek the Chinese Dream*, which is a wonderful work of art rich with connotative knowledge and artistic expression. In this poem, apart from his own talented poetic creation, he not only absorbs in the philosophic thoughts and poetic creams of hundreds of thinkers, scientists and cultural masters, ancient and present, at home or abroad, and also deseribes the development process of China in the past hundred years, and also demonstrates great challenges and rigid hardships China faced during the present hundred years or more, and also describes various representative figures who have influenced China's modern and contemporary histories. All this, so to speak, is but another tall mountain made of poetic art. After years of hard work, the great poem has finally been completed by means of Mr. Cai's decades of poetic talent, and with the Chinese Dream as the totem in his mind. Thus, Mr. Cai can securely be called "the Poet Yu Gong".

The evaluation standard of a poem deals not only with the number counts, but also with its quality and content. The high quality of *To Seek the Chinese Dream* lies in its superb complexity, in that it upholds the greatness and tenacity of the righteous heroes with lofty ideals during the seventy years since the foundation of the People's Republic of China though it is not the modern Chinese history and contemporary Chinese history; that it is rich with the historic deposit of the Chinese culture and with the focused illustration of the density and inheritance of the traditional Chinese Culture though it is not China's official history; that it echoed with the passion and rhyme of songs, enchanting the wishes and ideals of the Chinese people toward the whole world, though it is not the music; that it contains a lot of knowledge, figures and incidents in the Chinese history though it is not the textbooks of linguistics and history. The combination of all these elements, in the amazing talent and wonderful poetic techniques of Mr. Cai, has been derived into a great work with historical profoundness, philosophical thoughtfulness, political acuteness and artistic vividness, and with strong inspiration and attraction, which make the readers inwardly utter the admiration and pride toward the motherland, the Chinese people, the Communist Party of China, and Socialism with Chinese Characteristics.

Mr. Cai has intensively read the works by various figures such as Laozi, Confucius, Qu Yuan, Bai Juyi, Su Shi, Mao Zedong, Deng Xiaoping, Marx, Engels, Socrates and Hawking, and, what is more, he has also read the *Classics Quoted by Xi Jinping*. With careful disposition and wonderful conversion, he has put all the thoughts and arts of the sages and masters into inspiration, making our great nation shuttling aloft for good dreams along with the chanting of the poetic songs. And rather, it is China's modern and contemporary history with artistic rhythm, densely depicting China's great changes and rapid progress during a hundred years.

The long poem is composed of thousands of lines, with each line in seven characters, and with regular traditional rhyming patterns for a stanza or a group of stanzas. In content, the poem is like pleasant enchantment as well as colorful flowers. What is more, the poem covers every aspects of our nation: when it odes the people, it upholds their virtues and abilities, their thoughts for reform and their achievements; when it odes the incidents, it depicts great changes, dramatic progress and gradual developments. It sheds lights on today and future, integrating all the shining achievements since China's reform and opening-up into the poem. It also depicts the blueprint designed by Presiclent Xi Jinping into a wonderful today and future, and of universality and individuality. It is exciting to read as the follows.

> *By the coming of the year of twenty fifty,*
> *China will have been a paradise of beauty;*
> *Colorful flowers will compete in fragrance,*
> *The world will be in blazing magnificence;*
> *At that time China will stand out majestic,*
> *The world will admired her success realistic;*
> *China is blessed with truth, good and beauty,*
> *Like a fresh flower blooming in large bounty.*

This part of stanza, which is concise and resonant with lofty poetic passion, is taken from the chapter titled *Ode to the Genesis of the Chinese Dream*. China in the middle 21st century is vividly illustrated in this part with powerful expressions. The poem, which can be read or chanted, proves to be a work of wonder.

The expressions such as "abundant resources" and "heroic figures" are usually used to praise the wonderful things or persons in China. These are just generalized literary depictions, while Mr. Cai, in a creative thinking throughout his life-long consideration, has made his own way for the unique poetic expression, by which he covers China's whole territory in the time span of the recent hundred years, and, with various figures as the focus, collects all the figures and things of great value into the realm of China, as he sets lots of shining pearls into a beautiful picture. It serves as a new polymerization which is more descriptive than the general expressions of "abundant resources" or "heroic figures", delivering far-reaching associations to the philosophic thoughts, struggles, intention to reform, and pursuit for prosperity, all of which is used to ode to China.

> *Let me present you a cup of sorghum liquor,*
> *To strengthen the courage to further conquer:*
> *We dare to go deeper into the universe vast,*
> *As the Chinese people have united at last;*
> *We dare to take the Yangtze as a long ribbon,*
> *In furious tides we'll show our big ambition;*
> *We dare to hold the Yellow River to the Sky,*
> *In the energetic breeze we'll freely glorify;*
> *We dare to will the sun and the moon freely,*
> *And to call on the wind and cloud willingly;*
> *We dare to behave ourselves as a locomotive,*
> *With high-pitched tune we shall turn active.*

The above poetic lines are taken from the epilogue of the poem titled *Ode to the Duties*. It was created only by present-day Yu Gong, Mr. Cai, who has grown up by the Yellow River. In the old days when Cao Xueqin fought against diseases in a small cabin at West Mountain in the west suburb of Beijing, he created a book, the classtic famous novel all over the world. While nowadays, Mr. Cai, as a new Yu Gong, has been keeping himself lonely and solitary in his Dushu Study at the Cherry Garden for his colorful dream to depict China.

How wonderful is China with fertile land, tall mountains and long rivers! The days for revival of the Chinese nation will come soon, and long live China with the revival of the Chinese culture! Gazing at the vast sky with colorful ribbons waving and roam, I'll salute Mr. Cai, a new Yu Gong grown in the fertile land of China!

This serves as the preface for the poem.

December, 2017

自 序

求 索

蔡远方

  人，从历史中走来，最终归于历史。野火烧不尽，春风吹又生。历史是永不消散的记忆，永不凝结的思绪，永不断绝的新生。历史，不是复活亡灵，不是炫耀功业，是对出自大众并为大众献身的英雄的敬仰与怀念。这敬仰与怀念是史识、史训的重温与反思。鉴昨知今，足慰前人，足醒今人。

  对于中国百余年来轰轰烈烈的岁月，大众是多么感慨。多少期待，多少牺牲，多少失落，多少无奈，多少创举，多少革命，俱在这岁月的惊涛骇浪、风号浪吼之中。今日阳光普照，多少人年老体衰，多少人魂魄归去。后来者意气风发，气吞斗牛，奔赴前程，追梦筑梦。

  求索。建党是求索，建国是求索，改革是求索，追梦、筑梦亦是求索。求索，就是追求。而追求，就意味着有更新、更高的目标。珍惜求索，向着伟大目标进军。

  百年来，中国共产党人代代相传，如同火炬者接力，坚韧地跑着、跑着，跑向那奥林匹斯山的圣火。

求索，就是实践。马克思主义的发展史告诉我们，一定要提高实践的权威性，把裁判权真正交给实践法庭，由实践来对求索的成果作出抉择。不断地改革，就是不断地求索。

人类对宇宙不断地求索。霍金说："即使我们确实找到了基本定律的完备集合，在未来的岁月里，我们仍面临一项具有智慧挑战性的任务，那就是发展更好的近似方法，使在复杂而现实的情形下，能作出对可能结果的有用预言。一个完备协调的统一理论只是第一步，我们的目标是完全理解发生在我们周围的事件，以及我们自身的存在。"（《时间简史》）

求索精神是一种开拓精神。求索是艰难的，因为它"没有可以奉为金科玉律的教科书，也没有可以对中国人民颐指气使的教师爷"（习近平《在庆祝改革开放40周年大会上的讲话》）。求索精神是一种开拓精神。它体现了追求真理时的虔诚和执着，体现了创造开拓时的清醒和强烈。社会是在求索中发展的。在发展改革的道路上，除了求索这条崎岖的道路外，没有任何捷径。中国共产党的百年发展史，可以称为求索史，也可以称为创新史。求索是科学发展、社会繁荣的强大动力。

求索，就是希望。希望是长存的，但先要把握好现在；希望是走向世界的，但先要走向自己国家的人民。

宇宙在进化，人类在进步。在无序扩张的宇宙中前进，人类建立了一个从无序到有序的社会。中国改革开放四十余年，新时代开创者们不断地追梦、筑梦、圆梦，为此披肝沥胆。

作为诗者，我似乎探寻触摸到了新时代开创者们的灵魂，不禁拿起"英雄100"，饱蘸"英雄"墨水，用诗语咏颂时代英雄。

诗者，要经过心灵之砧的锻造。"自我"要成为一把钥匙，以开启别人的心灵。诗者的"自我"必须与读者的"自我"相沟通，否则，"自我"就丧失了任何积极意义。

1978年至2019年，中华大地改革开放，遍地生金。与"金"俱来的，还有多种多样的快餐文化。不能否认，快餐文化有一定的娱乐性，其中不乏优秀作品，但就其厚重度与可传承性而言，与中华优秀传统文化不可相提并论。快餐文化充斥坊间，优秀传统文化融于殿堂和山野。快餐文化裹挟着金钱与名利，迷惑着一些人忘了先辈，忘了肤色。承袭优秀传统文化，是珍重殿堂之神韵；供奉中华瑰宝，是敬奉先辈先烈之醒训。

中华民族从炮声中觉醒，在灾难中求索，在耻辱中奋进，造就了我们追求真理、坚定信仰、不怕牺牲、奋斗图强的精神品格。对真理和信仰的追求是不能马上实现的，但它的意义并不因此而丧失，而在于对现实的超越。它体现了人类追求至善至美的精神力量。如果没有这些伟大壮丽的、绚丽多彩的、为真理而奋斗的图景，一部人类的革命史、精神史、思想史将显得多么苍白、浅薄。

民族复兴，国家兴旺，人类和平，世界美好——是人民的愿望，亦是诗者的愿望，更是新时代开创者们的愿望。作为诗者，仅以此书，抒一抒胸中情怀，暖一暖英雄之心。

诗者以传统格律咏颂中华历史、中华英雄，亦是一种文学艺术的求索。诗者本着严肃和高度负责之心，将求索作品奉呈读者，旨在求索真理，追梦、筑梦、圆梦。

此为自序。

2019年春日，写于北京独书斋

Author's Preface

To Seek for the Better

Cai Yuanfang

Human beings, coming from history, will finally go back to history. As the grass cannot be burned out in the prairie fire and it will grow up again in spring wind, history is the never-die-away memory, the never-dry-up thought, and the never-broken life. History is not about the recovery of ghosts, nor the illustration of successful courses, but the admiration and remembrance of the heroes, who come from the people, and died for the people. The admiration and remembrance are review and retrospection to the awareness and lessons of history. The people alive nowadays can be self-examined by mirroring the past, which might console our forefathers.

How much the public feels about the great changes that have taken place in China in the past hundred years. All expectations, all sacrifices, all losses, all helplessness, all pioneering undertakings, and all revolutions, can be found in the rampant tides of the years. In these days when the sun is always shining, many people are staggering with old ages, many people are no more with us. The ones of the young generations, however, are energetic and ambitious for future creation and dreamy expectation.

We have been seeking: seeking for the foundation of the Communist Party of China, seeking for the foundation of the People's Republic of China, Seeking for reform and opening-up, and seeking for realization of the Chinese Dream. Seeking means aspiring, which aims for the newer and higher goals. Let's cherish such seeking and march for the great goal.

In the past one hundred years, the Chinede communists have been marching forward one generation after another, like torch relay, handed down from one to another, approaching to the holy fire on the top of Mount Olympus.

Seeking refers to practicing. The development history of Marxism shows us that the authority of practice must be upheld, that the authoritative power must truly be delivered to the count of practice, and that the sought achievements must be judged by practice. Continuous revolution means endlessly seeking.

Hunanbeings have endlessly been exploring the universe.Hawking says, "Even if we do find a complete set of basic laws, there will still be in the years ahead the intellectually challenging task of developing better approximation methods, so that we can make useful predictions of the probable outcomes in complicate and realistic situations. A complete, consistent, unified theory is only the first step: our goal is a complete understanding of the events around us, and of our own existence." (*A Brief History of Time*)

Seeking is an opening-up spirit. It is difficult to seek for the better, as it "has no authoritative doctrines to abide by, nor any supervisors giving orders to the Chinese people" (From *Speech at the Meeting Celebrating the Fortieth Anniversary of Reform and Opening-up* by Xi Jinping). Seeking for the better is a spirit to open up, in that it embodies the piety and persistence to seek for the truth as well as the awareness and intensity of creation and development. The society is developing along with seeking exertion. On the way of development and reform, there will be no shortcuts except the zigzag path of seeking. The one hundred years of development history of the Communist Party of China, so to speak, is a history of seeking for the better, or a history of innovation. To seek for the better, we'll have strong motivation for scientific development and social prosperity.

Seeking for the better refers to wishing for the best. Wishing is long lasting, and it should hold fast the present. When we wish the world the best, we should at first wish people of our nation.

The universe is evolving, and the human beings progressing.

Marching forward in the disordered expansion, the human beings have established a society from disorder to order. During forty years of China's reform and opening up, the pioneers of a new era have been seeking, creating and realizing the Chinese Dream, for which they have been taking great pains.

As a poet, I seem to seek and touch the souls of the pioneers of a new era, and I can't help holding my pen with a brand of Hero 100, using the ink branded Hero, and chanting the present heroes in poetic form.

A poet should be forged on the anvil of the soul. "Ego" should be a key, with which to unlock others' souls. The poet's "ego" must be well connected with that of the reader. Otherwise, the "ego" will be deprived of any positive significance.

The period from 1978 to 2019 has seen reform and opening up bringiny huge economic benefits to China. Together with the success, there has mushroomed a great variety of fast-food culture. It's true that the fast-food culture has something of entertainment, or even brings about certain excellent works. As far as the intensity and inheritance are concerned, it is quite inferior to the excellent traditional Chinese culture. The fast-food culture roars noisily in shops and bars, while the excellent traditional Chinese culture roams in the majestic halls and wild countryside. The fast-food culture , which crazes for money, fames and profits, has alienated some people to forget about their ancestors, their nationalities and their souls. Inheritance of the excellent traditional Chinese culture means cherishing our ancient culture spirit, and admiration to the precious Chinese treasures means keeping in mind the admonitions of our forefathers.

The Chinese people have awoken in the cannons of the foreign invaders, explored in the disasters, and exdeavored in the humiliations, all of which has forged us with such spiritual qualities as persistence for the truth, firmness in our belief, volunteering for sacrifice, and struggle for the stronger. There is a long way to seek for the truth and belief, but its significance is still available in that it lies in the fact that it will transcend the reality. It embodies the human beings' spiritual strength to seek for the good and the beauty. Without the picturesque visions, majestic, splendid and colorful, which mirrors the struggles for the truth, the human history of revolution, of spirit and of thoughts, will for sure be pale and shallow.

It is the expectation of the people, the poet himself as well as The pioneers of the new era to see our nation reviving, our country booming, the human beings living in peace, and the world keeping fine. As the poet, I just intend to express my emotions and to warm the heroic hearts.

The traditional rhyming pattern has been chosen by the poet to ode Chinese history and heroes, which is also an effort to seek for the better in literature and art. With a high sense of serious responsibility, the poet has dedicated the poetic work to the readers with a view to seek the truth, to seek and fulfill the Chinese Dream.

Such is my preface.

Dushu Study, Beijing, in the spring of 2019

目 录

引　言	追梦篇	001
第一章	筑梦篇（上）	015
第二章	筑梦篇（下）	033
第三章	天下篇	053
第四章	法治篇	073
第五章	修身立德篇	091
第六章	为政廉政篇（上）	109
第七章	为政廉政篇（下）	133
第八章	敬民笃行篇	155
第九章	育人任贤篇	173
第十章	战略思维篇	197
第十一章	新时代篇	213
尾　声	敢当篇	237
跋		246
后　记		250
致读者：关于《追梦》注释的几句嘱语		260

Table of Contents

Preface	Ode to the Pursuit of the Chinese Dream	001
Chapter One	Ode to the Genesis of the Chinese Dream (I)	015
Chapter Two	Ode to the Genesis of the Chinese Dream (II)	033
Chapter Three	Ode to the World	053
Chapter Four	Ode to the rule of law	073
Chapter Five	Ode to Moral Cultivation	091
Chapter Six	Ode to the Incorruptible Government (I)	109
Chapter Seven	Ode to the Incorruptible Government (II)	133
Chapter Eight	Ode to Hearty Respect for the People	155
Chapter Nine	Ode to Decent Education and Sound Official Appointment	173
Chapter Ten	Ode to Strategic Thinking	197
Chapter Eleven	Ode to the New Era	213
Epilogue	Ode to the Willing Duties	237
Postscript		248
Epilogue		254
Note to Readers Regarding the Notes of To Seek the Chinese Dream		261

引言
Preface

追梦篇
Ode to the Pursuit of the Chinese Dream

（第一节）

莽莽昆仑飞彩凤，
浩浩东海舞巨龙；
华夏雄狮显本色，
五彩云霞染碧空；
煌煌中华千古盛，
泱泱九州展大鹏；
尧舜禹汤周朝颂，
农耕之国乐农耕；
诸子百家群贤涌，
礼仪之邦倡文明；
五常仁义礼智信，
奠定东方大国风。
秦皇汉武长城固，
唐宗宋祖万朝迎；
成吉思汗雄天下，
弯弓射雕五洲行。

（第二节）

明清闭门弄风云，
西洋长天起大风；
文艺复兴前奏曲，
工业革命新文明；

(Section I)

As a phoenix is flying above the Kunlun Mountain,
And as in the vast sea there's arising a huge dragon;
China stands out like a lion holding its head high,
And like colorful clouds glimmering in blue sky;
As a big country prospering for thousands of years,
China sounds a huge miracle to whoever has ears;
Booming dynasties witnessed various kingly sages,
And farming was favored here in past long ages;
From hundreds of schools mushroomed the wise,
And thereby a nation of virtue dare to civilize;
Thus China stands up in the east as a model,
With her kind, just, polite, wise and sincere people.
The Great Wall was built in the Qin and Han Dynasties,
And in Tang and Song China attracted other countries;
When Genghis Khan swept the world with his bow,
He had emperors subjected with their heads low.

(Section II)

While Ming and Qing took China for the best,
Whirls of changes swept all over the West;
Renaissance came into being as a prelude,
And then Industrial Revolution followed;

改变人类命运史，
重读宇宙观天星。
苏格拉底柏拉图，
马恩先哲孔李翁。
俱是前辈大圣贤，
各有哲思育民众。
康梁变法求革命，
孙文黄兴覆清廷。
大钊先生著文章，
一九一七十月风；
手握长剑仰天啸，
南陈北李毛泽东。

（第三节）

百年中国百年梦，
万里长城万里征；
十三君子驾小舟，
英特纳雄耐尔鸣；
一九二一风乍起，
南湖涛声聚英雄；
一九四九十月一，
天安门上五星红；
一九七八冬似春，
三中全会国是兴；
廿一世纪春色展，

All this has made a new history of human fate,

And the world vision was anew at a great rate;

Philosophers as Socrates, Plato, Marx and Engels,

With Confucius, Laozi from the Chinese peoples;

Were all great sages from the former generations,

Who educated the mass with wise directions.

Kang and Liang held royal reform to be right,

But Sun Wen and Huang Xing urged the people to fight.

With the articles written by Mr. Li Dazhao,

China was inspired by the 1917 Soviet Model;

Heroes began casting their swords at the throne,

They were Chen Duxiu, Li Dazhao and Mao Zedong.

(Section III)

Like a dream China saw a century had passed,

There's a long way to erase hardships long-last;

A boat was launched with thirteen men noble,

China began thundered with the International;

The year of 1921 heard a whirl of revolution,

And the South Lake waved heroes to collection;

On October first of the year nineteen forty-nine,

A five-starred red flag was hoisted above Tian'anmen;

In the spring-like winter of nineteen seventy-eight,

The Third Plenum marks a turn glorious and great;

China began to bloom at the twenty-first century,

韶华正茂俊杰英。
壬辰辛亥庚辰日，
北京深秋枫叶浓；
蹉跎岁月磨利剑，
披肝沥胆双眸明；
先贤圣德参天地，
来者传承展新程。
马列主义是方向，
泽东思想指航程；
小平理论为指导，
三个代表记心中；
科学发展以引领，
胸怀壮志再长征。

（第四节）

百年岁月织一梦，
薪火相传若愚公；
代代英杰中兴绘，
字字珠玑笔笔嵘；
儒道育人胸广阔，
华盛顿公亦目瞠；
社会主义我本色，
中国特色大道通；
华夏传承五千年，
博大精深蕴文明。

When young talents swarmed in the old country.

On November the fifteenth of twenty twelve,

When Beijing was cool with crimson maple leaves;

The years of hardships tortured him mighty,

And his iron will made him acute with loft duty;

He has learned widespread from the virtuous sages,

Before succeeding and innovating in coming ages.

Directed by Marxism and Leninism all the way,

And by Mao Zedong Thought for the new journey;

And with Deng Xiaoping Theory as leading art,

He also keeps the Three Represents by heart;

And guided by the Scientific Outlook on Development,

He's launched a long march for better accomplishment.

(Section IV)

Hundreds of years has been woven into a dream,

As many true doers went all out for cultural beam;

And bit by bit they have made glorious history;

Heroes of various generations created prosperity,

By Confucianism and Taoism we've fine education,

Even Washington was amazed at our noble nation;

Since Socialism has been securely established,

The road with Chinese characteristics has been unblocked;

During five thousand years of the Chinese tradition,

There cultivated widespread and profound civilization.

霍金教授书简史,
郎达拜恩秘密衷;
百舸争流奋楫先,
宇宙精神逐梦争。
山河长卷细描绘,
妙笔生花起春风:
人民之梦中国梦,
国家民族人民情;
中国道路必须走,
中国精神必须弘;
凝聚中国众力量,
光辉彼岸唤复兴。
千年承载砺丹心,
百年屈辱心底横;
世纪奋斗为一梦,
九州大地龙虎腾;
建党建国大改革,
三大丰碑筑复兴;
哪有金科与玉律,
哪有师爷颐使令;
不可能为已可能,
创造伟大蕴民众;
一百春浩然高歌,
好儿女干云长空;
七十秋正气凛然,
九万里正举风鹏;

Even Prof. Hawkins wrote *A Brief History of the Time*,

Even Rhonda Byrne published her wonderful *mystery*;

We, too, should strive on like dashing boats in a river,

To work out the universal spirit for ever and ever.

Our native land should be depicted in a scroll long,

With vivid touches as spring wind comes along:

The Chinese Dream is the dream of the people,

The country, nation and people will always maintain a sense of unity;

The Chinese people must be on their own way,

And the Chinese spirit will never go astray;

The strength of China should be gathered totally,

And a culture Renaissance will come true finally.

For thousands of years we've born wills strong,

To crash our humiliations of hundred years long;

For this dream we've fought for a whole century,

And China has stood out to make a new history ;

By founding the Party and new China, and by reform,

China is reviving upon a higher and better platform;

We have no golden rules or ready laws to abide by,

Nor do we have any immortal supervisor to guide;

We can but get the possible out of the impossible,

As the greatness comes right from the great people;

One hundred years has heard the high-pitched song,

That the good sons and daughters have fought long;

Seventy years of righteousness has been ringing,

At a speed which a big space shuttle is bringing;

四十载惊涛拍岸，
中华史伟大改革；
创造飞跃再创造，
共产党人大觉醒；
改革方案一千六，
艰难困苦玉汝成；
注入鲜活生命力，
民族品格血脉溶；
生于斯而长于斯，
家园美丽宜人宫。

（第五节）

海岸远望船航行，
桅杆尖尖驾东风；
高山之巅眺朝日，
光芒四射喷薄升；
婴儿母腹乐舞动，
亦然果熟争黎明；
鲲鹏击浪扶摇疾，
艨艟巨舰似锦筝。
暾紫霞兮自东方，
夜皎美兮色已虹；
载云旗兮风卷云，
紫贝阙兮誉北京；
东方云海空复空，

Forty years of reform proves to be the magnificence,

Which has formed China's historical eminence;

China has been leaping from creation to creation,

And the CPC have brought this to animation;

Thousands of the reform programs are available,

And victories have been won with many a trouble;

Vitality has been injected in the Chinese nation,

Which would be inherited by the next generation;

Behold, this is the homeland for us all to live,

Which is our dreamy land if or not you believe.

(Section V)

If you look to the sea at the tip of a mast,

You will know that a ship is sailing past;

If you see that the clouds are golden,

The sun will rise to the top of the mountain;

If you find a woman is heavy with pregnancy,

It's evident that she will give birth to a baby;

You might see large sea birds scatter and flee,

Because huge ships are tilling the vast sea.

The eastern clouds seems to be blanched bright,

It is the neon lamps that beam at night;

The wind's blowing and the clouds flying,

The world's attention is paid to Beijing;

As groups of immortals appear with divinity,

群仙出没空明中；
荡摇浮世中国梦，
风卷处处友谊宫。

From the eastern world of vast virtuality;

The Chinese Dream has awakened the world,

Like a friendly wind whirling about wild.

第一章

Chapter One

筑梦篇
（上）

Ode to the Genesis of the Chinese Dream (I)

（第六节）

雄姿英发人生梦，
早生华发亦多情；
神凝长天五色展，
再启时代新航程。
丁酉庚戌戊寅日，
彪炳史册留汗青；
崭新共产党宣言，
中国特色新纲领；
战略总谱长歌颂，
豪气干云响九重：
二〇二〇目标至，
决胜小康民心腾；
二〇三五现代化，
美丽中国创新型；
二〇五〇国富强，
昂扬屹立天地中。
思想闪烁十三篇，
真理力量大无穷；
天下将兴积有源，
堂堂天道阔步行；
沧海横流显砥柱，
万山磅礴看主峰；
时来天地皆同力，

(Section VI)

Each one wishes to be successful when young,

And grey hair emerges due to the passion strong;

All under heaven are gazing at a colorful goal,

As there again has started journey new and novel.

On October the eighteenth of twenty seventeen,

History saw the 19th National Congress of CPC begin;

The Communist Manifesto was reviewed anew,

China has new-featured guiding principles to bestow;

The overall strategy was gloriously put forward,

Which illustrates a majestic expectation upward;

If our aim is obtained by the year of twenty twenty,

China will enjoy herself with decisive full prosperity.

And twenty thirty-five will see China's modernization,

Our beautiful nation will contribute to a new creation;

Twenty fifty is to see China rich and powerful,

The old country will be shown proud and youthful.

Behold the thirteen works with shining wisdom,

The truth of which can overthrow any kingdom;

They are the very source for universal booming,

By which paradise of China will come into being;

Seas of hardship will tell who is the true man,

And the mountains can show the highest one;

Common efforts are exerted at the due time,

运至方显大英雄；
莫让百姓留遗憾，
誓把祖国变富强；
坚持方略十四言，
兴旗定向引复兴；
坚定不移奔前景，
兴党强国气恢宏；
伟大政党敢胜利，
伟大政党敢斗争；
烽火成钢铸辉煌，
长征励志似图腾；
打铁必须自身硬，
天下为公大道行；
不要人夸颜色美，
留得清气贯长虹；
新时代圆中国梦，
新思想启国复兴；
气吞山河壮丽诗，
义无反顾使命膺；
伟大梦想即实现，
伟大斗争不懈停；
伟大事业党指引，
伟大工程众成城；
凝聚筑梦磅礴力，
不忘初心方始终。

And chance will tell who is great and sublime;

All the Chinese people have a great expectation,

Xi Jinping will make the motherland richer and stronger;

Only adhering to the ready governing manner,

We are to realize Renaissance under his banner;

Be steady and firm for our wonderful future,

And China will be strong and our Party mature;

CPC has proved to be a great political party,

In that she can boldly fight for final victory;

Chains of frustrations have cast into glories,

And the Long March's vitalized new stories;

To conquer the strong, we must be stronger,

To serve more, we are not selfish any longer;

We'll do nothing merely for admirable vanity,

But we'll give the world with clear nobility;

The new era will see the Chinese Dream come true,

And China will be animated by new thoughts, too;

A blueprint has been drawn out magnificently,

And it's our duty to put it into practice presently;

When the great dream is to be realized rightly,

Unremitting struggles must be launched tightly;

The great course is directed and led by the Party,

The great project should be done by all as a unity;

Mighty powers will be gathered for the Dream,

And we'll go all out at our original and final aim.

（第七节）

灯火万家奔小康，
唯是信念方为根；
秋风爽爽如春雨，
立志摆脱新平庸。
实践谓之理论源，
善于聆听时代声；
时代谓之思想母，
实践理论永探寻。
源清流清源浊浊，
上清下直社稷兴；
最大公约同心圆，
石榴籽籽紧紧拥；
创造创新勤铸就，
中华文化铸魂灵。
加强创新国体系，
保障改善惠民生；
加快生态体改制，
建设美丽东方城；
中国特色强军路，
红色基因永传承；
一国两制皆统一，
民族命运握手中；
和平发展共同体，
政设贸资民心通；

(Section VII)

Each household is marching forward for prosperity,

On condition that faith must be held in sincerity;

Autumn breeze is blowing pleasant and cool,

We are determined to avoid the deeds of a fool.

Practice is called the source of the theory,

We should listen well to the era's new story;

Time is the mother of thought,

Practice is the source of theory.

A clean source will lead to a clean stream,

An stable nation is lead by a clean team;

The team of CPC will lead to the common deeds,

Like the tight concentration of pomegranate seeds;

We'd work harder for creation and innovation,

To cast the soul for culture of Chinese nation.

An innovation for our system is strengthened,

And people's burden in daily life is lessened;

Quickened is ecological institutional reform,

A Eastern miracle is at hand in charming form;

With Chinese characteristics our army is strong,

The gene of Red Army is already handed down;

Taiwan is sure to be reunified with the Mainland,

And we'll grasp our national destiny by hand;

There'd be a community of peaceful development,

For which we can enjoy the common advancement;

零度容忍严治党，
海晏河清朗朗明；
三大历史任务重，
新时代谱新人生。
精英俊才扶庙社，
天地神灵齐贺声：
鹰击长空C919，
鱼翔潜底航山东；
首台光量计算机，
又探海域可燃冰；
琼楼玉宇在人间，
把酒问天乘我风；
高处言寒俱往矣，
有风有雨亦有情；
郎女千里共婵娟，
无须择日劳天公；
风流儿女尽风流，
出师一表荡苍穹：
太阳啊太阳太阳，
复兴啊复兴复兴；
中流击浪千堆雪，
江山如画画中兴！

The political party must be strictly disciplined,
And a just society will for certain maintained;
There're three historical tasks great and heavy,
In the new epoch as our mission compulsory.
All heroes should try hard for our country,
And for the graceful celebration by divinity:
China-made airliner C919 is high flying,
And our newly-typed submariner is diving;
Photon and quantum computers are to be,
And Combustible ice is explored under sea;
China is turning into such a land of promise,
That our forefathers may exclaim in surprise;
Gone is the past disillusion of eternal peace,
Now we can enjoy mortal prosperity in ease;
If Cowboy wants to see Weaver Girl today,
They are very easy to cross the Milky Way;
Here the lovers can enjoy the romantic love,
And the Chinese ambitions can shuttle above:
O the sun, the sun that has ever been shining,
O our rebirth, for which all China is pursuing;
China is like a ship dashing in the sea furious,
Till our land becomes a picture miraculous!

（第八节）

山海尽头远勿届，
志之所趋方向明；
穷山巨海不能限，
坚忍不拔助苍生；
志以发言言以信，
信以立志志以灵；
古之事者非唯才，
人须立志则建功；
上下求索承载重，
子魂魄兮为鬼雄；
奉公为民民为上，
愈挫愈勇敢牺牲；
路漫漫兮其修远，
只怕不懈登巅峰。
石可破也不夺坚，
丹可磨也仍赤红；
天授坚赤俱来性，
非能择取任意更；
我是谁乎为谁乎？
依靠谁乎应辨明；
共产党人有属性，
凛凛正气信念撑；
沪行兴业石库门，
嘉兴南湖红船红；

(Section VIII)

Let's go rightly for our noble ambition,

Even it is far away in a distant horizon;

Bare hills and deep seas cannot ban us,

To aid the mass we have courage surplus;

Our will makes us call out in hot loyalty,

And loyalty drives us firm in spirituality;

History says only talents do not suffice,

But he in firm will can make difference;

Let's go forward with heavy responsibility,

Even we someday die in noble immortality;

For the people we'll be readily unselfish,

For any cost we've our duty to accomplish;

There is a long way to go before our aim,

High on and we have no worry to exclaim.

A stone cannot be make bent even smashed,

As our blood is red even if we're crashed;

Everything is bestowed with its own nature,

How can we deform ourselves under pressure?

Who am I? And for whom am I willing to be?

And on whom can I rely? All this we'd see;

Such is the member of the Communist Party,

That he is righteous with a conviction hearty;

On Xingye of Shanghai, in a Shikumen building,

And then on a red boat in South Lake of Jiaxing,

孕育诞生共产党,
圣地重游寄后生;
烟雨楼台星星火,
红船劈浪聚人心;
大风泱泱云云起,
大潮滂滂潮潮涌;
乔木亭亭倚盖苍,
栉风沐雨自担承;
穿越时空遥呼应,
红色信念亦升腾;
依水行舟开天地,
母亲轻舸载众生;
不忘先辈强国梦,
铿锵誓言彻长空:
遵章履务拥纲领,
执行决定志忠诚;
共产主义献终身,
逢春蛰起殷殷声。

(第九节)

兴国之魂寓民众,
强国之魄寓青春;
百万青年百万胆,
一寸山河一寸金;
苟利国家生死以,

The Communist Party of China came into being,

Which has animated revolution of human being;

She lit holy sparkles into the dead misty night,

And she marched on like a flagship for fight;

Like fierce hurricanes stirring heavy cloud,

And like turbulent tide water roaring aloud;

Like a tree aloft up to the blue sky towering,

Against wind blowing and rain showering;

There is still an echo of the past fiery day,

The red faith will never be dropped away;

A new world has been opened up there,

And the mass need supporting with care;

We'll never forget our forefathers' dream,

To strengthen China as our eternal aim:

Let's get along with the party doctrine,

And be faithful to keep each disciplined;

We'll contribute to Communism forever,

And our ambition thunders up wherever.

(Section IX)

The people are eager to be nationally strong,

And the ideal of prosperity relies on the young;

Millions of youth are million-fold of bravery,

Each patch of land is rich of fine discovery;

I can exert all my strength and all my duty,

岂因祸福避趋行？
我以我血为人民，
民族精英民族魂；
晨光最耀八九点，
青春之歌贯长虹；
自强不息天行健，
厚德载物地势坤；
君子自励运不息，
顺天而动法天行；
刚毅坚卓力求进，
跋涉不挠强自尊；
敢有作为敢担当，
明知有虎虎山冲。
富贵不淫称豪杰，
威武不屈真英雄；
贫贱不移大丈夫，
秉持信念指南针；
居之天下之广居，
立之天下正位承；
行之天下之大道，
莫师春秋伪纵横；
怀抱理想坐标系，
超然纯粹为人民。
理想彼岸沧海横，
乘长风破万里行；
雄关漫道真如铁，

For my nation I can bear any responsibility.
I'll shed my blood for my beloved people,
And I'll stand out as a good example;
Like the morning sun bright and brilliant,
I'll let my youth burning to a full extent;
True heroes will constantly self-improve,
Virtuous men require no titles to prove;
A true man will try for better endlessly,
He will never go astray or act aimlessly;
Be iron-willed, and he will go for better,
Be self-esteemed, he's sure of his behavior;
Be bold in action, and keep ready on duty,
And be active regardless of any difficulty.
A hero won't be lured by worldly luxuries,
And a true man never bends to authorities;
Poverty can not change his noble mind,
With great faith he is firmly determined;
Since we are living in a greatest country,
We should keep ourselves as noble gentry;
And to act as a model to people elsewhere,
We should stand righteous now and here;
Cherishing in our sincere heart with ideal,
We'll serve the people with purest cordial.
The ideal is far away across the vast sea,
And by boat we'll cover ten thousand *li*;
The pass is grand and the march so long,

人间正道天有情；
八骏日行八万里，
碧海青天照征程；
直挂云帆济沧海，
举国圆梦借东风。
待到二〇五〇时，
九州犹如七彩虹；
百花吐艳争芬芳，
光照寰宇气色清；
那时华夏巍然立，
享誉世界唤大同；
天耀中华真善美，
山花烂漫笑丛中。

Heaven will bless us with a mind strong;
The sun is rising and setting day by day,
Shining in sky on our marching journey;
With sails high we'll cross the vast ocean,
In spring wind we'll reach our destination.
By the coming of the year of twenty fifty,
China will have been a paradise of beauty;
Colorful flowers will compete in fragrance,
The world will be in blazing magnificence;
At that time China will stand out majestic,
The world will admired her success realistic;
China is blessed with truth, good and beauty,
Like a fresh flower blooming in large bounty.

第二章

Chapter Two

筑梦篇
（下）

Ode to the Genesis of the Chinese Dream (II)

（第十节）

两个一百是愿景，
奋斗目标方向明；
小康社会亦展望，
富强现代指日成；
美好生活需努力，
艰巨繁重大工程；
前无古人伟大业，
任重道远信念增；
政治建设筑根基，
经济建设固民生；
社会建设祥云展，
文化建设舞彩虹；
生态建设绘美景，
五位一体总工程；
安得征程驰捷报，
满宇凯歌奏前门。
中国改革红利大，
波澜壮阔数十春；
深化改革扩战果，
湖水秧田荡绿村。
四个全面战略布，
言简意赅精辟深；
深化改革不回头，

(Section X)

The two centenary vision is our expectation,
It is clear to guide our endeavor and exertion;
A society of common prosperity is in our sight,
And a strong and modern China is in first flight;
A good life needs our exertion of great pains,
And great efforts should be taken for big gains;
The great course proves to be unprecedented,
To our firm hands the great duty is presented;
The political construction forms a foundation,
And what's vital is the economic construction;
The social construction ensures a vivid tableau,
And cultural construction as a colorful rainbow;
The ecological construction gives pretty vision,
And the five constructions are an overall mission;
We hope for the arrival of news on great success,
And cheerfulness will be burst at the front access.
China's reform has brought profits thick and fast,
Scales of years witnessed achievements at last;
And reform should be deepened for further aim,
For it's time that picturesque rural scene came.
There are four overall strategic assignments,
Which are concise but profound in contents;
We shall go all out to deepen China's reform,

万民小康乐万民；
依法治国定国是，
从严治党是根本；
试剑丹崖秋隼疾，
碧海江天水一泓。
四个自信壮行色，
坚持自信不放松。
坦坦荡荡行天道，
道路自信任我行，
理论自信代代颂，
制度自信信心增，
文化自信丹心耿，
历尽百折仍向东；
四个自信定风珠，
任尔东西南北风。
豪杰义士重名节，
心如丹石性如铿；
伯夷叔齐采薇去，
不屑武王威势汹；
吕氏春秋赞夷齐，
推崇气节太史公；
固然九死犹未悔，
终刚强兮不可凌。

Till all people's prosperity come in full form;
China is to be governed according to the law,
And strict discipline for the Party is the core;
Let's try hard through any harsh challenges,
And seas of victories will be sure in all ages.
We'll be strengthened with Four Self-esteems,
Which will be enlightening in constant beams.
The universal law will be candid to show,
We are confident of the route by which to go,
We are sure about our theory for which to ode,
We are certain of our system as excellent code,
We are heartily esteemed for our good culture,
And we will go forward in spite of any torture;
The Four Self-esteems will make us steadfast,
With which we can resist any severe blast.
The righteous heroes usually cherish fames,
And their hearts are attached to noble names;
They would rather live poor and miserable,
Than submit to a king mighty and intolerable;
We have many heroes highlighted in history,
Each one will last long in his virtuous story;
Though all of them as heroes finally died,
Yet their iron wills dare to never be defied.

（第十一节）

强军可期改必成，
人民军队浴重生；
脱胎换骨现代化，
上天入地皆悟空；
加强前瞻与探索，
战力创新科技争；
军民融合大战备，
试看天下谁争锋。
强军兴军长城永，
听党指挥是灵魂；
利剑藏鞘光亦闪，
剑出刃利卫和平；
百战百胜是核心，
作风优良是保证；
主席阅兵朱日和，
巨龙啸啸云霄冲；
千年底蕴炼丹田，
雄狮吼吼铁鹰腾；
今日长缨握在手，
百年圆梦志中兴；
不负先烈英雄梦，
不负代代殷殷情；
天若有情天若美，
蓝天白云永鸽鸣；

(Section XI)

The military reform is surely expected to be,

And there comes the rebirth of people's army;

Each modern soldier will become a new one,

Who is qualified for war and second to none;

Prospective exploration will be strengthened,

And scientific innovation also be deepened;

The army and people are united in case of war,

We turn out to be as invincible as ever before.

To strengthen and modernize our PLA army,

The key is to follow the command of the Party;

Even in sheath a sharp sword is shining,

And once drawn out, it's ready to cutting;

It's a law that our army is forever invincible,

And the sound discipline makes it possible;

Behold Comrade Xi's inspection at Zhu Ri He,

Fighters swarming above are superb for sure;

With long-lasting courage gathered within,

Our mighty PLA soldiers will never give in;

Today's China is seeing a military power,

And the China Dream will again recover;

We shall never let our forefarthers down,

Nor shall we betray our people old and young;

The vast heaven will be moved if it is alive,

And even the white cloud is flying like a dove;

但使龙城飞将在，
父老孺幼得安宁；
锦襜突骑待江渡，
安得娘亲乐田耕。

（第十二节）

经略海洋强国梦，
人海一体涓淙淙；
以海强国蓝天碧，
依海富国利民生；
莫疑松动要来扶，
经天纬地自身挺；
海浪时节华章颂，
肝胆宁忘枫叶红。
建设长江经济带，
横跨九州中西东；
长江经济是杠杆，
战略作用做支撑；
三角辐射以引领，
海上丝绸衔互动；
连接南北大走廊，
黄金水道大功能；
南雁归来北燕去，
迎客西游送东行；
大江东去浪滔滔，

Only if they ensure China's prosperity and peace,

Can the Chinese people live in happiness and ease;

Each peace-loving knight is ready for his shield,

Which makes their parents happy in the field.

(Section XII)

A great China should be strong at over the ocean,

Letting it become a part of organic dimension;

Exploitation of the sea will make us strong,

And the profit of the people will last long;

We should march forward without doubt,

And should be confident to explore about;

At the very time when we are strong at the sea,

China will be as prosperous as she can be.

We'll build Yangtze River Economic Belt,

A national booming will immediately be felt;

With Yangtze River economy as a lever,

A strategic role will be played for ever;

The triangle radiation plays a leading role,

And the sea route is applied as a whole;

The south and north is tightly connected,

And function of golden channel is exerted;

All travelers can conveniently come and go,

And cargos can be transported to and fro;

The Yangtze River is flowing eastward,

斜照江天一抹红。
粤港澳建大湾区,
优质城市互联容;
建立紧密经贸联,
打造世界城市群;
构建先导新格局,
改革前沿再升腾。
沪粤津闽四宝地,
三大经济水晶宫;
自由贸易试验区,
重大举措国际通;
长江珠江京津冀,
连接世界五洲行;
细听春山秋雨爽,
改革声声鹊鸟鸣;
故国风流今重来,
手种绿荫来日成。
文化一脉京津冀,
半径相宜相互融;
地缘人缘皆一体,
承载北京雄安城;
打造优美生态区,
建设绿色现代星;
发展高端新产业,
优质服务呈公共;
构建快捷交通网,

Reflecting the red sun setting westward.

There emerges a Big-Bay Economic Zone,

With Hong Kong and Macau linked to Guangdong;

By *Closer Economic Partnership Arrangement*,

A group of metropolises are in advancement;

A new pattern is designed ahead of fashion,

The reform has been fronted with passion.

With the eastern coastal zones favorable,

Three economies are assigned profitable;

There mushroom trial areas for free trade,

The markets attracts international aids;

Various areas and zones in our vast country,

Have linked to the world in the 21st century;

Listen carefully! The magpies are chirping,

As if they're singing for reform developing;

China will see her rebirth of fate grandiose,

And efforts should be exerted on our toes.

Beijing, Tianjin and Hebei are culturally one,

Having united, they'll prove second to none;

The favorable elements of Beijing in the future,

Have been gathered in Xiong'an as a mixture;

A beautiful ecological zone is to be laid out,

And a modern green star city is coming about;

To be developed are industries high and new,

Fine service will benefit people many or few;

Effective transportation net is in construction,

推进体制改革风；
扩大开放全方位，
对外合作献新容；
照日深红暖见鱼，
连溪绿暗晚藏虹。
以小见大展愿景，
以小带大寸寸功；
以上率下身先卒，
以上督下爱心诚；
踏石留印步步稳，
钉钉精神事竟成；
抓铁有痕破顽症，
壮志凌云铁肩承；
天生我才必有用，
前门一笑大江横；
立足九百六十万，
心怀全球展我胸。

（第十三节）

一带一路神来笔，
奇思妙想化鸽声；
安得丝路进万家，
炎黄歌儿动人听；
一叶舟上一支曲，
一带风采一路情；

It can push systematic reform as stimulation;

The all-round opening-up will be expanded,

And foreign cooperation will be newly landed;

The fish are warmly bathed in the red sunlight,

And a rainbow is hidden in a brook of dark light.

The great prospect can be perceived in little bits,

And the little bits will in turn give rise to profits;

As a leader, he is charging on ahead of any other,

As a supervisor, he treats his men like a brother;

Step by step, he is leading us forward steadfast,

Bit by bit, he's accomplished everything at last;

With toughest hands, he is apt to fight an anti-corruption war,

And in lofty will, he's taken his duty at a call;

Heaven for sure creates him for noble missions,

And he will laugh at a sea of severe tensions;

Standing steadily on China's vast territory,

His heart is filled with an earnest for victory.

(Section XIII)

Belt and Road innitiative is so wonderful,

That talented ideas have turned to deeds peaceful;

The Road leads to most regions of the continents,

Where the people will enjoy China's achievements,

One boat is related to one song with certain fashion,

One belt of grace accompanies one road of passion;

鱼群纷纷伴左右，
波涛滚滚来助兴；
一带一路神奇梦，
比翼双飞海陆风；
依托天赐梦之旅，
沿线丽城做支撑；
东西南亚印度洋，
华夏欧洋俱延通；
社会主义大胸襟，
善待资本不相轻；
惠及国际各国朋，
唤起世界护劳工；
西洋公约崇自由，
联合宣言亦可称；
近平丁酉党宣言，
宇宙精神不世功；
琵琶钢琴各指法，
双双重奏交响鸣；
西君开锣我奏乐，
我奏佳乐君鼓应；
你方唱罢我登场，
戏法各变妙不同；
美好世界人人爱，
人人爱护人人拥；
天公莫怪游人众，
谷莺海鸥皆鸟铃；

Shoals of fishes are accompanying on both sides,

And sharing the excitement in the roaring tides;

Belt and Road is a miraculous dream,

By land and sea we will manage a sound team;

Aided by Heaven we'll start a dreamy journey,

Along the line we are supported by each city;

From the regions of the Indian Ocean and Asia,

We can connect China to Europe and Australia;

Our socialist country is of generous pattern,

We cherish capital from the eastern or western;

We'll do favor to friends of other countries,

And appeal the world to keep their dignities;

Liberty is highlighted in the Atlantic charter,

And is also called in the international unities;

In 2017 Xi Jinping restated *the Communist Manifesto*,

Reveaiing the universal truth by which to do;

Pipa or piano, with typical musical instrument,

We both have different symphonies to present;

No matter if the music is from the East or West,

The harmonious performance is surely the best;

Let's make an art exhibition on the same stage,

Each artistic flavor must be on a different page;

The beautiful world is universally cherished,

And everyone can get our duty accomplished;

O Heaven, don't mind our being populous,

All songs of orioles or mews are euphonious;

香火缭绕旗脚转，
舟陆共有美酒迎；
至人有心无厚薄，
独有茶香和谐茗；
急促弹兮鼓对鼓，
翘吹竽兮撞编钟；
吟诗词兮会节舞，
心绪飞扬鼓角鸣；
乐哉五洲四洋友，
中华翔鸽驭东风。

（第十四节）

皇天后土佳橘孕，
橘树生来水土容；
橘生淮南则为橘，
橘生淮北枳为名；
根深蒂固难移植，
色彩鲜艳果肉清；
劲枝横展绝不媚，
横而不流俗不从；
浑身美丽花锦簇，
独立挺拔四季青；
清醒独立大地上，
胸怀宽广意定凝；
谦谦君子挑重担，

With burning incense at fluttering banners,

Fine wine is bestowed in friendly manners;

The sage leader is ready to greet to us all,

We are treated with fine tea of quality tall;

Drum to drum, we give a ready performance,

Flutes after bells, we play with magnificence;

Poems are being recited with beautiful dances,

We are of high spirits on such artistic chances;

With friends all over the world we are happy,

As pigeons of peace are flying in our country.

(Section XIV)

In the world orange has a unique feature,

That it grows in accordance with nature;

In South China it for sure is real orange,

But in North China, it's something strange;

By nature orange tree can't be transplanted,

Only in its original place can it be planted;

Its branches vigorously stretch in dignity,

And it keeps to its own life for prosperity;

It looks beautiful and noble in full bloom,

And in four seasons it continues to boom.

He stands on the land with a clear mind,

Broad is his chest for wills of each kind;

He bears the heavy burden with modesty,

固有大志意诚诚；
长江黄河共滋润，
永不凋谢绿叶荣。
穷不失义士得己，
达不离道德尊崇；
穷善其身修于世，
达善天下泽苍生；
天下无道卷而怀，
今逢盛世仕则行；
内圣外王崇尚品，
祖国梦圆致中兴。

And he holds his will in superb sincerity;

He is vitalized in every part of our country,

And his course will last century by century.

Even in poverty, a true man is but righteous,

And he must be of virtue when he's glorious;

He keeps himself noble in lack of chance,

And benefits the whole people at once;

He dare to recede when there was no way,

But he'd go all out in the booming day;

Being virtuous, intelligent and authoritative,

To realize the Chinese Dream is his motive.

第三章
Chapter Three

天下篇
Ode to the World

（第十五节）

己所不欲勿施人，
东方西方皆准绳；
西方道德黄金律，
东方一恕混天成；
推己及物话朱熹，
孔圣绝字终身经；
守望相助同舟共，
携手而济求共赢；
中非欧美发展梦，
梦梦相连梦梦通；
道义优先秉公道，
万物并育不相轻；
计利当计天下利，
求名应求万世名；
山积而高泽积长，
和而不同物之情；
浩浩渺渺行无极，
波浪扬帆但信风；
茫茫云山过海半，
遥遥目眺曙霞东。
茹毛饮血田园耕，
农业工业信息城；
多姿多彩文明谱，

(Section XV)

Both the East and West hold it as a law,

That one can't be forced against his will;

Virtue is the golden criterion in the West,

And in China general mercy is the best;

For Zhuxi, one must be self-disciplined,

And Confucian doctrines be underlined;

We should keep helping in cooperation,

Going abreast for a win-win destination;

China, together with the other countries,

Shares and enjoys the same prosperities;

Righteousness should be justly prevailed,

And the interests of all be fairly equaled;

Let's benefit all the people under heaven,

And let's earn the fame for eternity even;

We'll develop by gradual accumulation,

And naturally co-work in differentiation;

Though we have a long, long way to go,

Yet we all are energized from head to toe;

Just throughout the seas of misty troubles,

We are looking forward to great apostles.

From farming in the primitive condition,

We've the agro-industry by information;

Our civilization is patterned colorfully,

激荡史册气恢闳；
人类多元互借鉴，
阳光绚烂七彩虹；
沙漠无边多荟萃，
大洋广阔四海容；
一花独放不是春，
春色满园万花红。
以水济水无人食，
琴瑟专一无人听；
鼓瑟鼓瑟和且湛，
奏出美妙乐音声；
天空更比海洋阔，
虚怀若谷比天空；
不同文明互汲取，
琴瑟琵琶交响鸣。
道路并行不相悖，
万物并育不相争；
天地之光无不覆，
日月运行四时更；
人之欲望切适度，
一条小溪一涓淙，
一座山上一支歌，
一方水土一方宁；
宇宙天行自然法，
和合之道尽包容。
圣人不积以为人，

And our progresses recorded historically;
Man should learn from others in variety,
And the world can be shining in diversity;
Boundless deserts have become green,
All seas are connected in the vast ocean;
Only one flower cannot make up spring,
Which refers to whole garden blooming.
Merely with water a person cannot live,
And a single harp is not played attractive;
With the musical instruments together,
Can one prove to be a better performer;
The sky is much vaster than the ocean,
Which is smaller than heart of a person;
Civilizations benefit from one another,
As piano and *pipa* harmonize together.
All roads extend without contradiction,
And all things grow with harmonization;
Both heaven and earth are of full light,
Year in and year out the world is bright;
Man should be moderate in his desire,
As a small brook covers a certain area;
As one can't sing two songs meanwhile,
Only down-to-earth peace is worthwhile;
We have the natural laws in the universe,
And all should possess their fate diverse.
A sage will do everything for the people,

既以为人己愈丰；
既以为人己愈多，
利而不害天道行；
乐助人者人恒助，
圣道重为而不争；
春秋赋君情义重，
亲诚惠容中华情。
知之则强不知老，
是为同出不同名；
愚者不足智者余，
愚者求异智求盟；
千枝万叶叶叶秀，
不见两片叶相同；
凝聚共识求大约，
差异之曲亦同工；
平等相待互尊重，
共享机遇挑战迎。

（第十六节）

中国特色经济学，
开拓当代新进程；
农为基础工为导，
国际国内市场兴；
两种资源互为用，
促进社会臻公平；

And by this means he has set an example;
He's found himself rich for good of many,
And by benevolence to the human destiny;
The helper will earn consistent assistance,
And a sage won't compete in any instance;
Highlighted in ancient China was fraternity,
Together with favor, tolerance and sincerity.
With such virtues we will be much stronger,
And with the laws we will be much younger;
The wise people will live in great abundance,
And the stupid be tortured in opposite stance;
All trees are growing toward the certain aim,
There aren't two leaves completely the same;
They can be generalized in a rough similarity,
And there's for sure something of peculiarity;
In equality we should show a mutual respect,
For the common good opportunity to expect.

(Section XVI)

Economics with the Chinese feature,
Has opened a new era in the future;
With agri-basis and leading industry,
Markets are rising from our country;
We have used two kinds of resources,
To promote China's social justice;

细读论语资本论，
中国特色慧无穷。
明者固时而变通，
智者随世而制行；
因循守旧不适时，
与时俱进不世功；
近有润之心之力，
远有桓宽盐铁论；
历史长河运昼夜，
世间万物变换中；
古今大贤照后世，
今日我辈当谨从。
世易时移事则异，
事异世异变则通；
昨日是而今日非，
今日非而后日行；
逝者如斯不昼夜，
东哲圣人亦有云；
西哲赫拉克利特，
亦云不能两次同；
打破思维固定势，
更新理念顺势应；
把握创新新规律，
时代前列大步行；
信念不变应万变，
顺势而为方向灵；

Reading *The Analects* and *the Capital*,
One can trace in China what is vital.
The sages should be in-time prime,
And the wise tend to go with the time;
Confining to cliched proves a failure,
And going with time leads to future;
Modern years has seen works by Mao,
Which can match the classics before;
The history goes on ahead day by day,
And everything changes without delay;
Behold the ideals that the sages pursuit,
All of us nowadays should follow suit.
As the time is flying on, all transform,
And the changing world needs reform;
Yesterday's truth dare to be error today,
And today's error be rightly display;
All will be gone like this day and night,
As China's sages have put it into light;
Heraclitus, the philosopher in the West,
Held that nothing can stand for a rest;
To break up the old pattern of thought,
We should renew our ideas to go all out;
We'll grasp the new law of innovation,
And march forward in great procession;
With firm faith we'd be ready for all,
And our response is made for any call;

玄奘不变灵山路，
无有悟空难取经；
金猴奋起千钧棒，
玉宇万里埃澄清；
胸中日月常新美，
世事时移动若明。

（第十七节）

事预则立无预废，
无备之举草率行；
热情能力不可弃，
方法选定事成功；
善其事者先利器，
敬奉贤者结其仁；
利器为助贤为友，
磨刀不误砍柴工；
改革进入攻坚期，
利益价值杂丛生；
钢琴美妙钢丝稳，
艺术智慧寓其中；
认真考量大系统，
切忌瞎摸胡折腾；
小处着手庖解牛，
着眼称象读曹冲；
欲横奔而失其路，

Determined as Master Xuanzang is,

He'd fail without aid of the monkey's;

The monkey ensures all with his weapon,

And the world is kept in good condition;

The sun and moon are new in our mind,

Everything in our life will be well defined.

(Section XVII)

Everything should be well-prepared before hand,

And unprepared deeds will give rise to no stand;

Enthusiasm and ability should not be abandoned,

By right means nothing hard dare to be burdened;

Success can be obtained by effective apparatus,

And fame and honor will go up to the generous;

Aided with tools and supported by comrades,

Victories will be conducted decades by decades;

As our reform comes to the stage with hardship,

Profits and values vary among the membership;

We should act readily like a finished artist,

Whose wise talent proves to be the worthiest;

The grand system must be examined seriously,

Rather than operate it ignorantly and blindly;

Each detail should be managed with precision,

And wisdom can be triggered out by imitation;

To run for more distance, one would go astray,

空叹韶华付流东。
天施气地化而生，
天施地生与时行；
其益无方无不在，
施化之益大无穷；
风雷相益迅则猛，
凡益之道能始终；
现实脉搏把握准，
战略思维眺远程；
洞悉潮流研趋势，
国际社会共识同；
和平共处五原则，
求同存异久而恒。

（第十八节）

是虽常是时不用，
非虽常非时必行；
用是失之不得时，
是非之理理不同；
桀纣幽厉失时败，
尧舜禹汤顺时成；
非行非时必然败，
非行逢时亦成功；
是行是时要逢时，
是不逢时功不能；

And would find him down with his hair grey.
Under heaven the earth is all alive with life,
And on the earth everything grows in strife;
The benefit is fully available without limit,
And the benefactor is even great in every bit;
Our progress bursts into being like thunders,
And our course will march on in good orders;
The impulse of our reality should be grasped,
And the strategic thinking will also be gasped;
To look on the developing tide and tendency,
The whole globe will act on the same policy;
With Five Principles of Peaceful Coexistence,
We should seek common ground while reserving differences.

(Section XVIII)

Eternal truth will be of no use at certain time,
And unproved ones will be somehow sublime;
Untimely, the truth will turn out to be a false,
And a single truth varies in a different course;
Tyrannies were failed when passing their days,
And the sage kings succeeded along due ways;
False deeds in undue time lead to sure failures,
And successes will go with untimely adventures;
Due time will make measures really workable,
And overdue undertakings are not profitable;

民谚兴啥啥不丑，
深刻至理寓言中；
大道亦言尹文子，
高山流水贤者清；
形势变化在发展，
正确错误变化中；
随时变化而改变，
是非标准亦变更；
阵地意识常不懈，
适时解决本领恐；
网络发展格局变，
是变非变是非明。
穷则思变变则通，
通则事物能久恒；
恒则事物亦在变，
变则永在发展中；
远古神农始创造，
黄帝尧舜禹继承；
通其变之民不倦，
神而化之民宜兴；
自天佑之无不利，
变者古今至理公；
世异事异则备变，
周邦虽旧维新兴；
近代维新变法涌，
农业之国得启蒙；

Rather true to life are sometimes folk sayings,

That many golden doctrines are in their findings;

Even a ordinary man can trace the Great Way,

And the noble persons will carry the evil away;

The situation are changing in the development,

The truth can become the falsity at any moment;

With time changing, there are various alteration,

And criteria of truth and falsity is in distortion;

We should take firm hold of the sense of struggle,

And problems will be duly solved in ways single;

In times of the internet great changes have taken place,

To change or not, we'd have a right way to trace.

Hardships will give rise to reform for the better,

In this way everything will go after the starter;

Even in eternity everything is not keeping still,

Only in constant changes can nothing turn ill;

Our earliest ancestors had the sense of creation,

It was handed down generation after generation;

With certain reform the people keep it actively,

And wise innovation makes it sound and lively;

Blessed by heaven everything goes on all right,

Long ago the sense of reform was kept in light;

Reform is ready at hand with world changing,

By reform, even an old country keeps booming;

Recent centuries saw China in tides of reform,

Enlightening the agri-country in a new norm;

菜市口闹六君去，
图变血染北京城；
世界万物始发衰，
恩格斯翁早言明；
社会主义常变化，
变化改革寓始终；
改革只有进行时，
通之变之无止境；
当今世界日月异，
民众需求日俱增；
莫负芸芸众期待，
改革代代沐春风。
国家治理大体系，
党社文生和政经；
规范法制民主化，
统一协调成系统；
治理能力现代化，
内政外交稳步行；
合理有节强效率，
科学光芒射朱梦。

（第十九节）

政党本根马克思，
学习服务创新型；
少知而迷乱本性，

It was difficult to reform in the nation of farmers,
And Beijing was shed with blood of reformers;
Everything will develop hard in the beginning,
As has been pointed out in Engels' wise saying;
There are constant changes in socialist course,
And through reform we have changes to cause;
Reform will be on the way for ever and ever,
We should keep changing for better and better;
Instant changes are stirring the world today,
People's demands are increasing day by day;
We'd go according to the people's expectation;
Before benefiting generation by generation.
The national management is a big system,
Including each aspect on governmental item;
Law system needs formalizing by democracy,
Forming into a system along with the policy;
We shall modernize our governing capability,
Putting domestic issues right with foreign entity;
By reasonable moderation for high efficiency,
We'll let science beame with complacency.

(Section XIX)

Marxism is the core of our Communist Party,
By learning and serving it attends a stage lofty;
One might go astray because of ignorance,

不知而盲无所从，
无知而乱陷困境，
加强学习塑心灵；
决策体现时代性，
科学预见主动行；
把握规律敢创新，
骐骥先路君驰骋。
发展理念日又新，
深刻变革筑本根；
发展潮流十三五，
引领未来注强音；
绿颜自然大底色，
民族生命凝聚深；
参木眉株齐努力，
山水苍茫碧殷殷。

Which would make him lost in turbulence;
Ignorance and turmoil lead to embarrassment,
And we should learn for spiritual enhancement;
Decisive policies show the temporal feature,
Scientific prediction leads to active venture;
We're grasping the rules for more innovation,
And we can march forward with wise direction.
The concept of development is daily changing,
Profound reform gets rooted in very beginning;
The Thirteenth Five-Year Plan turns out to be,
The most powerful undertaking as one can see;
With green as the fundamental color of Nature,
The whole nation will become one in the future;
Our country will be lively with trees tall or short,
Our mountains will be covered with green of any sort.

第四章
Chapter Four

法治篇
Ode to the rule of law

(第二十节)

法治中国是目标,
人民满意是标准;
社会主义法统一,
片片枫叶映民心。
依宪治国是根本,
人民当家做主人;
资本主义唯资本,
社会主义唯人民;
人民群众宪法定,
人民行为宪为准。
巡回法庭特色新,
全善中国法功能;
维护司法生命线,
纠偏纠祖为民诤。
杜绝暗箱不公正,
生效律文网上行;
规范法官裁量权,
决断权限进律笼;
职业水平新阶段,
正义凛然寓公平。
巡视制度反腐剑,
八府巡按察民情;
古有青天包文正,

(Section XX)

China is aiming at the law-based administration,

And the criterion lies in the people's satisfaction;

The laws of the socialist China should be unified,

Which may reflect what the people have required.

Governing by the Constitution is fundamental,

And the hosts of our country's are but the people;

Money is highlighted in the Capitalist countries,

And the socialist people are of unique dignities;

The people's rights are set by the Constitution,

Which should be taken as the people's criterion.

The circuit court is something of new feature,

It will perfect China's law function in future;

And it will maintain the dignity of justice,

And it can put the legal concept into practice.

With it the black case work will be abandoned,

And with it no criminal acts will be pardoned;

Judge's discretion will be greatly regularized,

And their decisive authority be standardized;

Their professional level becomes much higher,

And justice is blazing all over like prairie fire.

Inspection system is sharp for anti-corruption,

And tour judges can watch the civil condition;

As China would remember famous Judge Bao,

今有巡制护众生；
两责一律一传导，
震遏治本三功能；
祖龙魂系党犹在，
胆照华国树千丛。
法者是为法之端，
政治走向成熟中；
法治治国里程碑，
现代化之根本经。

（第二十一节）

国无常弱或常强，
有法有度国家兴；
奉法者弱则国衰，
奉法者强则国丰；
荆庄齐桓荆齐霸，
燕襄安釐燕魏雄；
荆齐燕魏称强盛，
皆因法度奉法行；
后君无度其国乱，
释国法而私其行；
国家衰落薪救火，
舍其国法私利营；
规章穿窿顶上拱，
唯有日积奉法风；

Today's people will be protected by inspection law;

By means of certain laws as well as regulations,

We'll take measures to hold social foundations;

With the Party's leadership as the very core,

Our ambition for a booming nation is more.

Legal system should be held by the law men,

And by the legal system our politics will ripen;

The rule of law serves as the milestone,

Our modernization will be sung by this tone.

(Section XXI)

Not a country is constantly weak or strong,

With the law and regulations it booms long;

A country is weakened with the law weakened,

And it is prosperous with the law strengthened;

During the time of the Warring States in China,

Such states as Wei were dominating year by year;

Other states like Chu and Qi were mightier, too,

As they focused legalized rule into social taboo;

Riots emerged because of latter kings' disorder,

They lost the sense of law for their own order;

There was no way to hold back their destiny,

And self intents replaced the law of country;

The law system serves as the vault of a palace,

No private intention dare to take the law's place;

日积月累拱心石，
构成坚实穹窿顶；
有效之法不刻石，
淌流民众血液中；
执法得利违法恐，
奉法者立信者众；
滋润冰心养玉壶，
敬奉法制红绿灯。
善法可使一国治，
善法可使天下兴；
一沐三发不给力，
一饭三哺力尽终；
推动天下广施教，
芸芸众生心刻铭；
善法要具根本性，
善法要观全局荣；
善法要使国稳定，
善法要能长期擎；
以人为本统筹顾，
为乘阳气适令行；
国家发展大有益，
善法才得善法名；
原样照搬不堪用，
中国特色中国情；
何须渡洋寻芳草，
独秀端砚磨丹青。

The effective law should not merely be printed,

But be what all the people have really intended;

Let law-abiders profitable and out-laws fearful,

And let the law-keepers supported by the people;

We should hold the sense of law most sincere,

And the punishment of out-laws must be severe.

Legalization can make a country well-disciplined;

And can make the international peace underlined.

Every measure should be taken effectively,

For legalization to be realized extensively;

Only when goes all abroad the sense of law,

Can the peoples hold it harder than before;

It's fundamental to maintain the law sound,

And with it an overall prosperity is found;

Sound law can maintain our country stable,

And it can make us developing sustainable;

All-round plan is made with Man as the core,

And work should be done for chances more;

It will benefit the development of our country,

With keystones accumulated for a period long,

The vault dare to be constituted firm and strong;

A good name and a good deed is in symmetry;

Mere adoption of others turns out to be no use,

Adherence to China's feature is a good choice;

We need not ask for law system from overseas,

For we have as many genius as everyone sees.

（第二十二节）

国家安定靠法制，
国家混乱私是根；
道法者治道私乱，
法立无人敢私徇；
法者国家治之本，
依法治国法度循；
国无常治无常乱，
行弛治乱法令遵；
去私行公兵强敌，
去私就公抚万民；
从严治党纪严明，
廉洁奉公秉忠心；
以言代法不可取，
以权压法民不尊；
徇私枉法千夫指，
私心作祟失万民；
行为自觉外以形，
道德自律内持忠；
善治境界道法治，
桃花园里吟诵声。
天下立法或不难，
难于立法法履行；
法律生命在实施，
法律权威在遵从；

(Section XXII)

A country is stable by means of legalization,

And riots mushroom because of privatization;

Without legalization no one can live in peace,

Unless the authority of the law is held at ease;

National administration is based on the law,

And legalized management brings sound rule;

A country tends to be legalized or non-legalized,

Only with law can the social order be realized;

Our army will be powerful by being non-private,

And our people comforted by being non-private;

The CPC should be strictly disciplined,

And faithfulness to the people be underlined;

The law should not be replaced with authority,

And pressure of law be despised by majority;

The abuse of the law will be cursed commonly,

And distortion of the law be abandoned openly;

By outer behavior one must abide by the law,

And one must be self-disciplined all heart and soul;

The best condition of a country is legalization,

Which will lead to prosperity of whole nation.

It's not difficult in China to keep legalization,

But it's very hard to put it into due realization;

The spirit of the law lies in its implementation,

And legal authority is kept by the whole nation;

言法不难难于效，
询事兴事考其终；
若无综核怀苟且，
尧舜禹皋亦难成；
尊其主权课吏职，
笃信赏罚一号令；
居正施行考成法，
奖廉惩贪查实名；
法治应为民信仰，
人民权益得保证；
人心才是大法治，
科学立法司公正；
建设守法好环境，
建设中国执法明；
沧海横流何足虑，
天安门前万妍红。

（第二十三节）

法令即行纪律正，
治国治民无不从；
法不明则难正纲，
无纲不足护公平；
纲弛不能张道义，
纲而不举目不撑；
人知法令不足信，

The core is its effect rather than talk about it,
And only in practice can we truly promote it;
Only when we treat it in a comprehensive way,
Even the ancient sage emperors would go astray;
Each legal official should be sure of his position,
All praise and punishment are in the unification;
Legal system must be truly examined in justice,
Corruption and bribe be punished in the practice;
The legal system should be admired by people,
And maintenance of rights be an good example;
The people's support serves as the basis of law,
And just law will cover everything big or small;
The good environment of law should be done,
And China's rule of law must be the best one;
We would worry about no challenges,
And our country is like flowers by Tian'anmen.

(Section XXIII)

Legalization can put in good order everything,
And a disciplined nation will come into being;
Without a clear law politics is out of the light,
Without political line we can not be kept right;
Righteousness will be gone in slack system,
And in this condition we'll spoil each item;
Mere a sense of law is not due and sufficient,

重在天下法提衡；
邪佞之徒必罢黜，
忠士虽疏应授用；
赏罚之典典遵循，
不可恩进应赏功；
罚者必须当其罪，
不可幸免污典恒；
国家安危之大柄，
令典律执风气清；
执法如山法制践，
共产党人师包拯。
治国之圆不失规，
方不失矩末如本；
为政应能遵其道，
方可兴业建功勋；
去冗就质除之虚，
闲闲无用蛀害隐；
绵绵不绝必结乱，
纤纤不伐妖孽群；
三纲不正六纪废，
失规失矩蚀国桢；
防微杜渐须警视，
无秩废序丛生根；
孔明便宜治乱策，
远内本强大写真；
近外末弱小不计，

The throughout disposition of law is important;
Evil and corrupted officials must be rejected,
And just and faithful ones be rightly appointed;
By the law appointment and rejection is done,
No one can be praised by private favor alone;
One should be punished according to his crime,
And no one is pardoned for his position prime;
Legal system is vital to the safety of a country,
Legal order will be indispensible in our society;
A firm legalization means put it into practice,
Our CPC members should be of great justice.
Our country will be ruled according to the law,
And strict abidance to the law is the very core;
Only abide by the law in our political actions,
Can we always prosper in various generations;
Each legal disposition should be down to earth,
Useless deeds lead to corruption underneath;
Interlaced errors will give rise to big riots,
And tiny misdeeds to monsters of big lots;
Without law everything will be out of line,
And our nation be ruined without discipline;
A huge tree is withered from the very root,
And a society corrupted with a slight loot;
As Kong Ming ruled the State of Shu nimbly,
The governance of the state was pictured simply;
By ignorance of civil issues which is trivial,

何来功业和道统？
法制根本系准绳，
法治思维法制炘；
上下对称规律论，
创业源泉涌流奔；
九州方圆天下秀，
日照长城万点金。

（第二十四节）

法立有犯而必施，
令出如箭不收弓；
法不行则法尊损，
破窗效应亦形成；
中国特色法体系，
适时必须严遵从；
令出若汗出不复，
朝令夕改切忌行；
王勃少年呈相书，
年未及冠敏而聪；
晁错贤良对策论，
一片至诚可烁金；
严程峻法绝轻陋，
奸镕之源源不通；
沿风正典重耕耘，
邪赢之计计无踪；

How can one conduct the feasts immemorial?
By the law people's life can be regulated,
And the conception of the law can be realized;
There must be law high and low in symmetry,
Enterprises will be booming in our country;
Our nation will be standing out prosperously,
As the Great Wall in the sunshine joyously.

(Section XXIV)

Any violation of the law must be punished,
No hesitation or delay once it is finished;
Otherwise the dignity of the law is gone,
And the legal items is destroyed one by one;
The Chinese legal system is of great feature,
Which must be abided by in term of Nature;
Every legal regulation should not be loose,
No violation is allowed as one can choose;
Wang Bo once wrote to the prime minister,
When he was a bright and talented teenager;
Chao Cuo commented on the good or evil,
His extreme faithfulness dare to surely prevail;
Yan Cheng held legalization in high authority,
Which made corruption disappear in reality;
Great exertion has been made in legalization,
And we live sound generation by generation;

远弘教旨变流俗，
窃者五刑田者功；
不负晁错心之愿，
不负王勃少年情；
落霞孤鹜滕阁拜，
秋水长天共回声。

By this means we'll better our social custom,

Letting men righteous from their heart bottom;

Only when the whole society is truly legalized,

Have Chao and Wang's wishes realized;

When all of us live in our country like paradise,

The whole world would gaze at us in surprise.

第五章
Chapter Five

修身立德篇
Ode to Moral Cultivation

（第二十五节）

为政之德是根本，
众星凝聚似北辰；
知行合一行天下，
立身立国净灵魂。
为仕之法惟三事：
日清日慎日日勤；
远离耻辱心洁静，
得上之知得下尊；
廉不言贫勤不苦，
爱其洁身修其心：
信仰意识本根固，
公仆意识为人民，
自省意识常反思，
敬畏意识如履冰，
法治意识践法令，
民主意识系灵魂；
自信人生二百年，
清慎勤勉日日新。
取法于中得其下，
取法于上得其中；
邪径或近而易践，
良由大道远难行；
夫惟病病以不病，

(Section XXV)

Virtue is the fundamental basis for politics,
And all the people can unite with this ethics;
All will work in line with theory and practice,
The whole nation have the morale to notice.
There are three fundamentals for the officials:
Which is clarity, cautiousness and diligence;
With the noble heart away from humiliation,
One dare to surely earn praise and admiration;
The incorruptible and diligent boast nothing,
And the good officials will come into being;
The sense of faith should get deeply rooted,
The idea of service should be widely booted,
Self-consciousness should always be in mind,
And the sense of awesomeness be determined,
The sense of the rule of law put everything right,
And the sense of democracy sheds blazing light;
It's evident that our life will last sound and long,
An incorruptible government will march along.
With less effort, we cannot accomplish more,
And for moderate progress we must go out all;
By going astray one tends to feel comfortable,
And by right road one feels much challengeable;
Only by encountering hardship one can win,

太宗帝范嘱子卿；
律己标准亦严格，
严格才能动力增；
放松标准泻千里，
确立标准高效能；
前人之法今谨记：
沧浪诗话严羽声。
一心丧邦皆为私，
一心兴邦然为公，
公私之毫见心性，
毫末之分显品行；
二程遗书传学道，
立品立德国家兴；
百年风雨共产党，
公私二字度量衡：
一心为公论操守，
二字为德何不赢？
众生所归为众生，
如旱望云驭临风。
重莫如国德如栋，
君修其心修其身；
化成天下臻佳境，
经世治国意充盈；
立德修德践德品，
为民务实清廉公，
立言立行俱统一，

As an ancient emperor decreed his son and officials;
One should be stern and strict in self-discipline,
Only by this means can we but for ever give in;
Slackness in criteria will give rise to frustration,
And with firm criteria we'll do it to admiration;
Of our former elders we should get their ways:
Wisdom dare to be sought even in the old essays.
By selfishness a country will be totally ruined,
But for the people a country can be maintained,
Their difference dare to be seen from the spirit,
Which can demonstrate who deserve it;
As two Chengs' works dare to convey the Tao,
High virtue can make China booming more;
In the past century with seas of big challenges,
The Communist Party of China met changes:
She undertakes everything in line with virtue,
And selfless orientation is not overdue.
True selflessness is for the people always,
As they look forward shower in the dry days.
What is most important in China is but virtue,
Cultivation of body and spirit should continue;
With the whole country cultivated as the best,
The ideal administration will endure any test;
We according to virtue should do everything,
And try hard to contribute on people's living,
One should keep his words to his very deeds,

朝雾琼宇沐晨风。

（第二十六节）

为官避事平生耻，
身负重任勇担承；
朔朔疾风识劲草，
烁烁烈火见真金；
勤勉任事不苟活，
忠诚之士亦忠诚；
克己爱人拯天下，
曾文正公治心经。
鱼之有渊人之忠，
犹如岩石海浪中，
良士守忠美名扬，
鱼不失渊人守忠；
蜀相诸葛书兵要，
恺撒大帝论忠诚；
对党忠诚生命线，
共产党员第一称。
君子不患位不尊，
惟恐谦谦法不崇；
德不厚者不使民，
德者立言亦立行；
不耻禄之夥与寡，
只耻智之不博通；

Which will be profitable for people's needs.

(Section XXVI)

It's shameful for an official to undo his duty,
But rather he should serve for his country;
Only tough undertakings can tell a true man,
Fiery burden can be as testable as one can;
One should conduct his duty diligently,
And also demonstrate his loyalty presently;
One should fight for the nation in discipline,
As Zeng Guofan kept his duties in good line.
One's loyalty has its origin in the beginning,
As a huge rock in the vast sea keeps standing,
A faithful virtuous man will get his fine fame,
And one should hold his faithfulness the same;
As Zhuge Liang stressed in his military works,
As Caesar the great stated in his imperil books;
It is vital to be faithful to the Communist Party,
Which serves for each CPC member as a duty.
A true man will not worry about his high post,
And he will be degraded once his duty is lost;
A person without virtue will not be an official,
The virtuous will say and do anything cordial;
One should never worry about more wages,
But about increase of his intelligence for ages;

捷邪之径不投步,
张衡应间语坚定:
间者非议诘难语,
不能夺君心之恒,
献身科学无他念,
不求利禄与功名。
廉不言贫方本色,
勤不道苦乐其中;
尊其所闻善中言,
行其所知力践行;
内乡衙联七百年,
翻缮几多楹未动;
风吹雨打百姓心,
已然铭刻云天中。

(第二十七节)

慧者心辩不繁述,
慧者多力不伐功,
慧者名誉扬天下,
慧者无惰志诚诚;
大智慧者首固本,
春秋墨子重修身。
定魂方能冥目静,
知止后定志向明;
魂静使得心儿安,

One can not go astray to pursue anything evil,

And stand fast for scandals serious or trivial:

Any gossiping talked by the mean persons,

For the righteous is mere reverting lessons,

One should think only of devotion to science,

And let alone profits and fame by conscience.

An official must be honest even in poverty,

And he must work hard as his innate duty;

He should go according to the moral rules,

And he should act in line with the principles;

See in Town of Neixiang the government buildings,

Which has nearly been changed by mendings;

This has earned firm support by the people,

And the officials were learned as an example.

(Section XXVII)

The wise can judge without words lengthening,

And he is also powerful not for other's listening;

The wise tend to be well-known under heaven,

And he is hardworking for his duty to fasten;

The man with top wisdom stresses the basis,

As Mozi in ancient China dare to avoid any crisis.

Only a steady stander can be truly tranquil,

And only a reasonable man dare to be not ill;

A rationally-minded man can be inwardly calm,

安后而虑神智清；
虑后精神方能得，
心浮气躁神难凝；
三关通畅砥砺志，
人间起舞弄清影。
国宝四维天柱擎，
礼义廉耻铸魂灵：
一维绝则大厦倾，
二维绝则危机萌，
三维绝则山河覆，
四维绝则灭我种；
国守民治四维润，
东方明珠火独明。
四慎防微不弃末，
祸咎莫于已欲膨：
权独微友四慎记，
手握戒尺日三省。
律己宜似秋风紧，
处事宜如裹春风；
君子与人不求备，
贤人检身若不及；
尚书伊训犹在耳，
居上克明为下忠。
欲而不止失其欲，
有而不足失其终；
一失足成千古恨，

By which he can dispose everything in his palm;
He'll be spiritually mighty in such consideration,
Otherwise he'll go astray in restless mediation;
He'll realize his ideal will without any obstacle,
Before he makes his undertakings into a miracle.
There are four fundamentals to govern the people,
Which are the ritual, righteous, honest and noble:
Without the one the country would be collapsing,
Without the two the social crisis would be rooting,
Without the three our country would come to end,
And without the four our humanity would descend;
China will be booming with the four fundamentals,
And the world will admire China in noble morals.
To keep the four fundamentals we'd do everything,
And in ill-desires disasters would be mushrooming:
Precautions should be done to keep us freshly alert,
And disciplines be kept for daily efforts to exert.
To ourselves we must be stern like chilly wind,
And we must care for other with our full mind;
A man of big virtue has nothing to over-blame,
And a generous person has but morale to claim;
The teachings in our classics are also present,
In that leaders be wise and subjects intelligent.
Unbridle desires will bring about big torture,
And excessive greed will give rise to failure;
Once a loss will lead to ever-lasting regret,

不义富贵如浮云；
老子嘱君春秋赋，
史记珍言再叮咛；
穿破欲海千层目，
输肝剖胆效英雄。

（第二十八节）

从善如登从恶崩，
古之大贤左丘明：
不以善小而不为，
不以恶小为我行；
映阶碧草自春色，
隔叶黄鹂妙声鸣。
见恶探汤躲恐恐，
见善不及追匆匆；
高比使君以广德，
下比使君以狭行；
论语点睛摘与君，
韩诗外传亦曾云：
坚持时时勤拂拭，
疾恶如敌善流从。
见贤思齐君子为，
不贤内省亦为君；
择善而从有我师，
不善而改益终生；

And ignoble man will have no honors to get;

All this has been warned by Laozi in old days,

And such golden rules must be set nowadays;

Let make it clear to fight against any ill-desire,

Then we'll be totally noble as the sages require.

(Section XXVIII)

To be righteous is like a man who is ascending,

As a famous ancient figure called Zuo Qiuming:

One should do anything good even if it is small,

But he should not commit anything evil at all;

The green grass at stage makes scene of spring,

And natural music is tree-hidden birds singing.

One should avoid the wicked as he the hell,

And he should seek the good when others tell;

One should compare himself to Emperor Liu Bei,

Who was famous for his virtuous deeds anyway;

There are some golden sayings in *The Analects*,

Which were also mentioned by other intellects:

One should always be keeping himself noble,

And be trying hard to get rid of anything evil.

A true noble man will learn from the sage,

Even the ignoble can be noble in courage;

One should learn from whoever is better,

Even a sinner will become a virtue-scatter;

贤小善恶君自辩，
莫听穿林打叶声。

（第二十九节）

疵瑕不滞观明镜，
听于直言不累身；
光阴造化钟神秀，
神韵尽来圣天隐。
宁静致远慈怀众，
宽大兼覆制断平；
淡泊明志砺心趣，
鸟系黄金难破云；
刘安主训淮南子，
泰格尔公言亦衷；
欲望过盛迷心智，
劝君目远心境明。
终始如一同心济，
信仰矢志君子朋；
革命理想比天高，
道义名节行志忠；
真诚友谊天地久，
同舟共济山水青；
专擅狭隘离散窘，
协力广博通畅成；
共志共荣共其利，

Only by oneself one can tell good from ill,

And become a man of virtue in iron will.

(Section XXIX)

With a mirror one can find dirt on his face,

And by honest words one goes by easy pace;

The due time will bring about the right leader,

And a chance is left to whoever works harder.

Only the quieter can go further for the people,

And the generous will win as a fine example;

The strong will can work only in a calm mood,

With heavy burdens one can do nothing good;

All this was recorded in *Huainanzi* by Liu An,

And also mentioned by Tagore, a sage Indian;

Over-excessive desires drive one out of mind,

And one should but let them gone with wind.

We will go all out at a goal common and grand,

With a firm belief we unite on the same stand;

The revolutionary ideal is supremely sublime,

And our morale for it will never prove slim;

The cordial friendship will for sure last long,

And our common course will be ever young;

The narrow-minded dictators will fail fast,

But the united mass is bound to win at last;

The victory comes from common exertion,

共道共功共其名。
以势交友势倾绝,
以利交友利穷终;
王通中说礼乐篇,
山高水长论真情。

And fames arise out of the fine cooperation.

True friends never care about the property,

And a sense of profit will harm their unity;

In "On Rites and Music" of *Zhong Shuo*,

And a truly happy nation will be long blessed.

第六章

Chapter Six

为政廉政篇
（上）

Ode to the Incorruptible Government (I)

（第三十节）

四个全面星棋布，
四铁标准铸中兴：
铁般信仰炼胆魄，
铁般信念润心灵，
铁般纪律金刚体，
铁般担当轻死生；
明明暗暗织伟业，
八柱矗立擎九重。
政治立场要坚定，
政治头脑要清醒；
守规讲矩党标准，
对党对民要忠诚；
道德至上明白人，
勇担善成铁铮铮。
党章党规是天道，
系列讲话融汇通；
党员是君身份证，
两学一做基本功；
身佩信符务民众，
芳香浓郁天下公。
政治生态需经营，
精心筑建好环境；
优良污浊人为事，

(Section XXX)

The *Four–Comprehensive* strategy has been organized,
And the *Four Criteria* will make it realized;
The iron belief makes us brave and bold,
And the firm will benefits us young and old,
The stern discipline keeps us in an integrity,
And we are dauntless with the sense of duty;
The great course comes from ups and downs,
And we are supported by our cities and towns.
We should hold steady in our political stand,
And be clearly aware of our political strand;
The sense of discipline is upheld by the Party,
To whom and to people we give our sincerity;
We should be aware of the priority of virtue,
And then our course will forever continue.
Divine is the Constitution and regulations of the Party,
Which, with series of speeches, are an integrity;
The Party membership is our very identity card,
And with this identity all of us must work hard;
With the holy identity we must serve the people,
And contribute ourselves as a shining example.
The political ecology needs due management,
And efforts are exerted for a good environment;
Its natural for a man to do things good or evil,

政治自然均相同；
吉日良辰今亦是，
浪沙淘尽道洞庭；
驾桂帆顺水飞渡，
跨越四海神舟行。
欲知方圆必有规，
欲知平直依准绳；
党的规矩寓刚性，
身先士卒模范行；
一江春水如歌咏，
波滔滔兮万民迎；
云气涌涌足下翻，
东风一飘万骏腾。
八项规定联群众，
工作作风系民生；
援北斗兮酌桂浆，
红军归兮五星红。
不谋私利亦权重，
权力关进制度笼；
君子位高不擅权，
以事民兮竭忠诚；
乘清风兮阴阳驾，
祥云缭绕滋众生；
云霞紫衣长长舞，
神龙播雨声声隆。

And the same is conditions of issues political;
Presently we met in China the golden days,
All hardships are gone in spite of some delays;
We'll rush on like a sailing boat in tail wind,
By which we can cover anywhere in mind.
Only with compasses can one draw a circle,
And only with a pen can he writes an article;
The Party's doctrines will not be neglected,
And good examples can be easily collected;
Our course is going on like a big spring river,
As it's aided by the people forever and ever;
Clouds are waving and floating at our feet,
And horses are racing for victories to meet.
The Eight Regulations link firm to the people,
And we will win along with our working style;
As a natural guide the Party benefits the mass,
Like the Red Army ranking the first class.
The public power must not be privately abused,
And unbridled power lets the nation confused;
A high official of virtue will not misuse power,
And he can put it aloft and keep himself lower;
He will devote day and night like a noble sage,
And keep benefiting the nation through his age;
Because of this our life will become colorful,
And the noble contribution will be wonderful.

（第三十一节）

虫众木折隙坏墙，
腐败源自不正风；
老虎苍蝇皆虫隙，
锦绣家园忌蛀虫；
姑息养奸心为祸，
杀尽贪官固长城；
塌方腐败令人兢，
惊首回望触目瞠；
二月河疾书雍正，
周梅森痛写忠诚；
和平北平无战事，
史醒后人叹介石：
遥想毛周刘朱君，
率领精英围北平；
兵临城下不血刃，
念念不忘庶百姓；
百姓是君英雄胆，
凝聚中华民族魂；
介石携带黄金去，
孤篷渡海别祖冢；
只识黄金失民心，
漂泊孤岛哀叹声；
夫释大道任小数，
神德不全劳无功；

(Section XXXI)

A group of moths can destroy a growing tree,
And corruption is the same as anybody can see;
A nation will be spoiled by cadres big or small,
Anti-corruption campaign must be waged at all;
The mercy on them will bring more disasters,
And the bad officials be punished in clusters;
We have been shocked by each bad project,
Which makes the everyone furious to object;
As in a novel titled *The Reign of Yongzheng*,
Corruption will endanger the imperial throne;
As mentioning peaceful liberation of Beijing,
Chiang was criticized for his corrupted doing:
When reminding of Mao and other PLA leaders,
Who had Beijing breached without ladders;
The City was seized peacefully without war,
Beijing citizens' contribution was the core;
For the leaders they are of heroic courage,
And it was they who pushed PLA to the stage;
Chiang went to Taiwan with all of his gold,
And lived in the tiny island till he was old;
With his gold he but lost support of people,
In Taiwan he puzzled his ruling principle;
A cunning leader will never become great,
And in lack of virtue he had nothing to treat;

润之恩来入燕京，
白手起家聚民众；
人心资本无限大，
不可斗量不可称；
君以人心凝华夏，
四洋五洲傲群雄；
沃土九百六十万，
亿兆民心指日腾；
淮南子嘱原道训，
肺腑谆谆醒诸公：
自我净化时不待，
苍鸟翔飞似雄鹰。

（第三十二节）

猎狐行动瞰大地，
天网行动震长空；
疏而不漏网恢恢，
避罪天堂地狱中。
权力清单制度新，
坚决清除寻租人；
作忠无视以怨恨，
正道不豫芳终身。
顾全大局恪守律，
内记于心化为行；
妄议中央非本分，

Since Mao and Zhou entered age-old Beijing,

China began to be united in very beginning;

People's support served as the most important capital,

Which is mighty with a power immeasurable;

By then China has been truly become a unity,

Which stands in world with majestic indignity;

With the vast territory of the People's Republic,

Millions of the people became fully energetic;

As is told in a classic work called *Huainanzi*,

A golden law is available for us to memorize:

Do not hesitate in self-refreshing,

And our national will be acting and booming.

(Section XXXII)

When the Hunting-Fox Operation has been launched,

The corrupted officials have been fatally punched;

A vast net of law against the wicked has been cast,

Only to the hell can the dreadful criminals get past.

The new system focuses on the definition of power,

Nobody dare to go on abusing his prestige forever;

A dutiful cadre will not be afraid of any hostility,

And a good official will be noted for his nobility.

One must look at the big picture and observe the discipline,

Keeping it in mind and put it into real action;

It's a fault to gossip on CPC Central Committee,

自身位置必摆正；
横越四海心有矩，
致力改革惦民情。
严以修身真君子，
严以用权大道通；
严以律己追先贤，
横四海兮翔云中；
谋事要实科学奉，
创业要实勇践行，
做人要实襟坦荡，
君欣欣兮兰做旌。
为官不为是重症，
无能懒思不担承；
执篲非人滥充竽，
长城累土终无终。
群众路线是基石，
教育实践重活动；
保持发展先进性，
务实清廉品纯真；
水流石滩波声溅，
横渡大江显神能。

（第三十三节）

县衙关键少数官，
省府关键少数君；

And one must not have his right stand go astray;

Throughout China the discipline must be kept,

And reform beneficial to people we must accept.

A strict discipline-keeper is a real man of virtue,

And a cadre without abuse of power is truly due;

One will be strictly self-disciplined by example,

And then he can be qualified virtuously capable;

We should do everything in a scientific way,

And only in practice can we carry all away,

Each one of us should be honest and candid,

By which our quality will be happily splendid.

It's fatally wrong if an official is of inactivity,

With this he would be slack in his responsibility;

If the government is occupied by such officials,

They would do harm to our Party's essentials.

The line for the mass should serve as the core,

By education we can highlight practice more;

We'd keep the advancement for development,

And are honest and genuine in management;

A small brook tends to get its water splashing,

And a big river but its tides quietly rushing.

(Section XXXIII)

A county government relies on the key official,

So is the cadres in the government provincial;

少数承担大责任，
劝君莫负亿万民。
县官要如焦书记，
赤胆忠心裕禄公：
心中有党恒心定，
心中有民百姓撑，
心中有责不懈怠，
心中有戒常自省；
一副铁肩一腔血，
一身正气两袖风；
四有书记遍天下，
四海五岳晏河清。
政者身正不令行，
其身不正令不从；
桃李不言自成蹊，
上行下效劲清风；
身先士卒率先范，
修身立德为政清；
登高远望山九仞，
聚焦聚力聚精神；
木秀于林风摧之，
大国治理赶考行；
甲申三百年谨记：
赶考莫学李自成；
滚滚江声走白沙，
飘飘云霞五彩迎。

As a few of them bear the great responsibility,

Thus they should work hard in full capability.

Each county leader should be like Jiao Yulu,

Who was the shining model for us to follow:

With the Party in mind he stood in firmness,

And all for people he earned respectfulness,

With a sense of duty he kept striving for better,

And he also kept self-cautious in any matter;

With cordiality he was active in his mission,

Being most righteous he earned admiration;

Once all our cadres learn heartily from him,

The Chinese nation will be ideally sublime.

By justice a leader can put all in good order,

But riots will bite the heels of an evil leader;

Without hot words the people can follow suit,

As he is a shining example for public pursuit;

Once he marches on forward as a locomotive,

The pure political exertions will be affective;

One can look further only if he aloft ascends,

And for success one must strive to the ends;

The out-stander would encounter jealousies,

And so hard is administration in big countries;

Taking the tragedy of Li Zicheng as an example,

Such bitter failure would let down the people;

The historical tragedy is gone with the wind,

And the awful lessons must be kept in mind.

（第三十四节）

为国生事如饮鸩，
为国畏事饮鸩同，
无病而药夫生事，
病而不服夫畏争；
东坡侃侃国是论，
主动作为敢担承；
遇事退缩不可用，
无端取事是非生；
治大国如烹小鲜，
心稳手准方见功；
基础扎劳步为营，
根深枝壮叶方荣。
安不忘危须谨慎，
存不忘亡临渊心；
治不忘乱常警惕，
否极泰来保国兴；
底线思维喜时忧，
临难静气定力沉；
坏处准备好处争，
永不懈怠国安宁；
野渡苍松横古木，
骤雨狂风仍从容。
苏轼亦书晁错论，
天下之患谨论心；

(Section XXXIV)

National trouble makers will bring disasters,

And the same are those who are lazy ministers,

Ridiculous are those who are ado about nothing,

And it's wrong for the evil to avoid correcting;

As is said by Su Shi in one of his political essay,

To any relevant affairs one should take it easy;

The duty-retreaters should never be appointed,

And the trouble-makers will let us disappointed;

Administration of a big nation is in a free hand,

Effective measure will work in the whole land;

We should go steadily forward pace by pace,

As a deep-rooted tree grows tall in any case.

In time of peace we must be aware of dangers,

And in good days we're ready to be changers;

We must be cautious of riots in time of peace,

And maintain our nation booming in great ease;

Even in happiness we'll be aware of the future,

And in disaster we'll behave as a nation mature;

In precaution for bad we should seek for better,

So as to keep alert forever as the peace protector;

Look at the green pine trees in the far wilderness,

Against pouring rain and wild wind in calmness.

As Su Shi said in his essay titled *On Chao Cuo*,

The national crisis comes from morale poor:

治平无事莫懈怠，
不测之忧时思忖，
坐观其变而不为，
恐至无救悔已深；
身前身后兴衰事，
皆有子瞻料如神：
崇祯皇帝成大统，
前朝弊端积生根；
君虽清廉又奈何？
积重难返梦难寻；
待到李闯进京日，
魂系景山心恨饮；
乾隆朝野扬扬得，
奢靡腐化吏沉沦，
文治武功成往事，
嘉道中落已然临；
智者见于未萌时，
研判早谋防患谨；
亚欧大哲神互通，
莎士比亚亦同云：
壮时欣欣盛极反，
草木蕃衍皆同人；
未雨绸缪御衰朽，
经略万年亦永欣。
太宗言国如种树，
本根不摇枝叶青；

We should always be alert in time of peace,
Sudden worries will be settled down in ease,
If we are inactive in face of the changes ill,
We will repent if it goes on against our will;
Of all the national affairs prosperous or not,
Like wise Zi Zhan we should dispose a lot:
Wise as was Chongzhen, an emperor of Ming,
Fatal collapses came from former corrupting;
Even if he was a prince capable and ambitious,
All imperial corruptions made him disastrous;
When Li Zicheng attacked Beijing the Capital,
By hanging at Jingshan he came to an end fatal;
During the imperial reign of Emperor Qianlong,
Wicked ministers made the Qing not last long,
All imperial feasts were but an empty illusion,
And the reign of Jia Qing met a big depression;
A wise can trace what is going on before hand,
By which to dispose everything at firm stand;
The same are the philosophers in east and west,
Besides them, Shakespeare remarked the best:
Declination tend to emerge in time of booming,
And it is true of trees and grass as human being;
Anti-corruption campaigns must be duly waged,
Before the long-lasting prosperity can be staged.
Emperor Tang Taizong once said of governing,
Which should be kept steady like tree-planting;

隋炀宫中尽美玩，
穷兵黩武民怨声；
天下兴讨烽烟起，
遂至灭亡成史训；
世民夙夜孜不倦，
徭役不兴年丰丰，
百姓安乐朝清静，
贞观之治兴史铭；
吴兢贞观政要记：
此中听得莺鸦声。

（第三十五节）

以实治之庶事旺，
以文治之奸敝生；
百职不修要政弃，
实治为政贵在行；
做人谋事创业实，
虚谈废务浮光影；
唐甄潜书论权实，
文则不实实则通。
毋贪毋忿毋急功，
蹇叔三戒奏穆公；
梦龙游记东周志，
宣王中兴三戒铭；
审明大小以而图，

Emperor Suiyang was so extravagant in palace,

That the people rued at the empire out of place;

When the uprisings in the empire mushroomed,

The cruel emperor got his fate deadly doomed;

Emperor Tang Taizong toiled on day and night,

With less forced labors all went well and right,

The people lived in peace and the count calm,

There arose a historical prosperity in no alarm;

As can be available in the historical document:

Both gales and crows dare to be in enchantment.

(Section XXXV)

With cordial devotion we'll create prosperity,

And in artful tricks all are but colorful vanity;

Officials out of duty will lead to deterioration,

And efforts can be exerted for an ideal nation;

Our course will be carried on in sure practice,

And empty talks deserve nobody to notice;

As effective power was studied by Tang Zhen,

Artful vanity should be ridded by dutiful men.

For achievements one should not be too greedy,

Great loss usually comes from being too speedy;

In *Records on the East Zhou* by Feng Menglong,

Are Three Commandments by King Xuanwang;

Before action one must judge if it is vital or not,

酌清缓急以而行，
衡权内外以而施，
连接上下以而通；
蹄疾步稳激流勇，
谋后而动静后行；
有条不紊清主次，
劈波斩浪乘长风。
未有而为察幽微，
未乱而治灭无形，
病成而药失先机，
病成而治渴掘井；
改革发展问题多，
发展成形勿放松；
着着先手明秋毫，
慎终如始了于胸。

（第三十六节）

政如农功日夜思，
细心谋事恒心成；
春夏播耘秋冬藏，
敏思其始成其终；
殚精竭虑造福祉，
雨雪风旱夙夜公；
春秋左传农喻政，
新语为政古今融。

And one should right dispose everything to allot,

Inner issues and outer ones should be in balance,

And items upper and lower be put in due stance;

A fast horse should trotting on more steady paces,

Well-planned deeds will go along the easy traces;

We'll put the primary and secondary in order due,

Our course will be like a fast boat ready to row.

All troubles must be solved from the beginning,

And all riots should be put down before rooting,

A disease with delayed remedy will not be curable,

And an unduly treatment proves not to be workable;

Problems have arisen in reform and development,

And we should try hard to put them in management;

Precautions must be acutely prepared before hand,

Which from beginning to end we'd well understand.

(Section XXXVI)

Politics is like farming cultivation day and night,

And we must be careful to put each detail right;

As the crops sow in spring and harvest in the fall,

We should be aware of the whole process at all;

Efforts must be exerted for people's well-being,

And to all cases we must be selflessly devoting;

Politics was looked as farming by Zuo Qiuming,

And throughout history unaltered is its meaning.

政令适时百姓一，
贤良悦服顺时成；
六畜生育皆兴旺，
节令种植草木兴；
天时地利与人和，
皆因人为而顺通；
社会自然调阴阳，
群道得当万物逢；
中国道路中国走，
中国奇迹中国兴。

Timely political orders will make people as one,

By which a united nation will be second to none;

All flocks and herds will be growing quite sound,

And grass and trees will be planted all around;

All the favorable conditions and human element,

Will be available because of joint arrangement;

All contradictions will be adjusted in our society,

In co-existing Tao all grow well in great variety;

China will march forward along her own way,

With the China Miracle all doubts will go away.

第七章

Chapter Seven

为政廉政篇
（下）

Ode to the Incorruptible Government (II)

（第三十七节）

天下之耳耳贵聪，
天下之目目贵明，
天下之心心贵智，
万人操弓弓弓中；
广开言路博采众，
人心若齐泰山崩；
万家灯火系百姓，
思广目远倾耳听；
愚公移山志不懈，
齐心协力美梦成。
天下无不可为事，
审度时宜虑定行；
大贤成功先于始，
图者锐始必善终；
动有章法心有谋，
思维定势渐形成；
思维定势亦发展，
发展变化与时应；
解放思想总开关，
推动改革大进程。
青年和仲策略论，
文章出手四座惊：
利害之际不失常，

(Section XXXVII)

The people should be the best and acute listeners,

And they would be the most qualified observers,

They as the whole would be the most intelligent,

Given a chance, they would prove to be most diligent;

If their opinions are heard and adopted joyously,

Even the earth would be removed unanimously;

The people's well-being is of vital importance,

And their demands must be met in an instance;

Let us contribute our exertion in perseverance,

And our mutual devotion will be an ordinance.

With this, nothing in the world will hinder us,

And we'll duly have each obstacle to surpass;

The first step is of vital importance for a sage,

For a final success we'll go all out in courage;

We'll put all in order with a ready disposition,

Till a habitual norm comes over to formation;

A fixed thinking pattern is also in development,

Which will surely be in change in each moment;

Take the main handle of ideological liberation,

And we'll promote reform course to admiration.

There is a young man whose name is He Zhong,

And who's written an amazing assay before long:

The assay is related to necessities of the strategy,

大事之际不乱神，
麋鹿兴左目不瞬，
泰山崩前色不沉；
胜者有力自胜强，
不惑于后谋前矜；
墙苇头重根底浅，
山笋嘴尖腹中空；
君临大事而不乱，
定力四忌重之魂：
一忌朝令夕来改，
二忌急者难求成，
三忌自以为是者，
四忌眼高手低人；
突破四忌之误区，
保持清醒意从歆；
途见白云如晶海，
沾衣晨露玉树临。

（第三十八节）

一厘一毫民之膏，
一丝一粒君之名；
取一文则不值文，
宽一分则受之民；
廉政实伤应自律，
交际之常与谁云；

By which we dare to give exertions in wiry energy,

Any restlessness will not affect our concentration,

And sudden crisis will not bring about confusion;

The winner will stand out because of his might,

And he will not be puzzled by if wrong or right;

Weeds growing on the wall are not firm to root,

And a fresh bamboo on the hill is weak to shoot;

In face of the urgent issues one must stand still,

The four may-nots can make things done by will:

First, political rules may not be changed casually,

Second, the restless may not gain much usually,

Third, one may not be excessively arrogant,

Fourth, one may not be proud but incompetent;

If one dismisses the four aspects of shortcoming,

He dare to keep clear-minded in his programming;

Then each cloud he sees is like the pure crystal,

And he with morning dew is like a tree immortal.

(Section XXXVIII)

Every bit of wealth belongs to the folk people,

And each leader must be honest as an example;

To greed for a bit means an awful degradation,

And to be generous means to earn admiration;

One should fulfill his duty by self-discipline,

Only by consciousness can he be in a due line;

欲水不遏则自溺,
贪火不遏则自焚;
理想滑坡可致命,
信念动摇气节穷;
既行遵道而得路,
夫唯捷径以步窘;
大错铸成悔之晚,
小节不慎大节黩;
苟非吾有毫莫取,
禁止馈送张伯行;
纵蝇为害养虎患,
猛药去病重典刑;
刮骨疗毒士断腕,
习式风格替天行;
岂恐余身之惮殃,
唯念国与大厦倾;
为官不贪真君子,
为党不叛大英雄。

（第三十九节）

谦得益彰满招损,
忧劳兴国逸亡身;
祸患常积于忽微,
智勇由此所溺困;
一枚铁钉失马掌,

One would get drowned if he is lost in water,
And he would get burned if he falls in a fire;
The collapse of ideal will be seriously fatal,
The loss of duty will ruin him little by little;
For right aim one should go by a right way,
A short-cut would for sure let him go astray;
It's too late for one to weep for his big fault,
And a tiny error will lead to a dooming result;
We should be hand-tied if it's not deserved,
And we must keep discipline as if observed;
A sin will let us out no matter how big it is,
And only wonder drug can cure each illness;
We'd cut off an arm when bitten by a snake,
This is Xi Jinping's approach for us all to take;
To save our life we have to sacrifice the few,
A slight hesitation will bring a disaster anew;
A true official is a gentleman honest and clean,
And a hero would know what faith does mean.

(Section XXXIX)

Modesty is beneficial and pride is harmful,
And a booming course is from acts dutiful;
Disasters usually result from carelessness,
And wisdom will be drowned in slackness;
A nail gone will hurt one heel of a horse,

一只马掌失战神；
一匹战马失一战，
一战痛失一国城；
欧阳痛修五代史，
博斯沃思战役训；
古今中西莫能外，
握卷明史正党伦。
善禁之君先自禁，
不善禁者先禁人；
清风清气自身正，
八项规定反四风；
为官不正牛掉井，
制度莫成稻草人；
身儿不正影儿曲，
若安天下先正身；
申鉴政体藏古训，
魏澂亦曾上书云：
求身而不以责下，
尽己而不以尤人。
吏不畏严而畏廉，
民不服能而服公；
廉则使吏不敢慢，
公则使民不欺卿；
年富官箴刻石语，
廉生威则公生明；
藏污纳垢廉何在，

And a horse heel wounded will lose Ares;
The wounded horse brings loss of a battle,
And the lost battle means the fall of a castle;
The bitter lesson has been historically held,
And also showed in War of Bosworth Field;
It's nearly the same in both China and West,
Historical lessons make our Party the best.
A good national leader is of self-discipline,
By this means he'll keep others in good line;
The sound politics comes from self-control,
And the Eight-Point Decision serve as the tool;
An unrighteous official will be evilly trapped,
The system is not a puppy artificially capped;
Good reputation comes from the good deeds,
Morale must be set firm before one succeeds;
As a classic doctrine is recorded in *Shenjian*,
And also viewed by Wei Zheng, a wise man:
To others a self-disciplined will not be strict,
And a good official be forgiving in his district.
Awesome are the officials without corruption,
And respectable are he who has a full devotion;
The corrupted will not be respected heartily,
And the selfish will be despised thoroughly;
As Nian Fu had a rule inscribed in the stone,
The corrupted and selfish will stagger alone;
How can an official be good with hidden sin,

暗箱何来谈公平？
古兮三后之纯粹，
唐尧虞舜正光明；
美德无瑕群贤绕，
效法先贤乐民生；
夏桀商纣之猖披，
结党小人适时逢；
背绳墨以追邪曲，
竞相苟且取容丰；
共产党人之本色，
堂堂正正坦荡君；
伏清白兮以死直，
真操芬芳洁白情。

（第四十节）

侈肆则使百恶纵，
俭约则使百善兴；
文帝崇尚勤约俭，
文景之治奢凋零；
敬策之声汇心语，
联璧格言寓持躬；
清则百毒不侵体，
清则凛然气充盈，
清则心境趣高雅，
清则万众一心同。

And how can he be just with the deeds plain?

Purely honest were the Three Kings ancient,

With Yao and Shun as special enlightenment;

Good virtue will bring forth the talented men,

And happy livelihood is from sage's direction;

As for the wicked tyrants in China long ago,

Who would bring about men mean and low;

Without the law the evil-doers will go astray,

And in extravagance they'd be carried away;

Lo! The members of the Chinese Communist Party,

Are of candidness, righteousness and honesty;

Each one of them keeps pure till the end of life,

With good qualities for the noble and loft strife.

(Section XL)

Various evils come from rampant extravagance,

And modesty is like flowers with big fragrance;

When Emperor Hanwendi promoted modesty,

His reign witnessed a country in big prosperity;

Hearty remarks are given for the sound politics,

And chains of wise sayings are held in classics;

Be uncorrupted, and one will be virtually fine,

Be uncorrupted, and one will be in a right line,

Be uncorrupted, and one will be inwardly noble,

Be uncorrupted, and one will win all the people.

奢靡之始危亡渐，
漆器不止必为金；
金亦不止当为玉，
美玉流行奢侈风；
古有诤臣褚遂良，
不卑不亢谏太宗；
奢靡腐败同沉滢，
同气相投相伴生；
渊源源于权谋私，
中饱私囊慷慨公；
蜂蛾微命力何因，
煌煌青天念民生；
共产党人宗旨明，
体察众生秉衷情；
一权谋私一家奢，
失去血脉失民心；
皇天无亲惟德辅，
芳香飘飘蜂自寻。
人必先疑而后谗，
物必先腐而后虫；
铁冠道人范增论，
自身疑腐显陈平；
必先而后两对比，
孰因孰果了然明；
内律失守惑自入，
理念动摇底线崩；

The downfall of a country is form extravagance,

Live-for-better ideas will occupy the intelligence;

From good to better one would craze out of mind,

And then one would go for the best of every kind;

There was a righteous official called Chu Suiliang,

Who persuaded Li Shimin, an emperor of the Tang;

Corruption comes side by side with extravagance,

The two, with the same feature, live in dependence;

Its origin is the profit-hunting by means of power,

By which properties are robbed of from the lower;

Even an insect has the divine right to live in Nature,

Thus the innocent people must not exist in torture;

The CPC members have their principle exact and clear,

The people's voices must be heard in an acute ear;

Whoever is for private profit will prove ruinous,

And they will be doomed in their fate disastrous;

Heaven will for certain bless whoever is of virtue,

In firm perseverance their nobility will continue.

Scandals would fly to whoever is suspected often,

And moths would ruin the wood which is rotten;

As was said by Fan Zeng, an iron-capped Taoist,

Together with Chen Ping, an ancient strategist;

One must catch hold of the truth by comparison,

And the cause and result will be in an illustration;

Sins will arise when the inner discipline is gone,

And collapse will encounter the corrupted one;

信仰迷茫神缺钙，
怎抵惊涛拍岸声；
锻造金刚不坏体，
百毒不侵如苍松。

（第四十一节）

纵览家国论古今，
败落由奢成由勤；
开元之盛唐事兴，
玄宗丧失进取心；
遥听骊宫青云乐，
仙歌飘飘处处吟；
渔阳鼙鼓动地响，
惊破霓裳羽衣魂；
骄奢淫逸挥无度，
盛衰弹指一瞬临；
骄傲怠惰溺享乐，
安史之乱写长恨；
唯其清廉挡横欲，
何须琥珀方为枕；
激浊扬清第一义，
养廉美德是其本；
荡去滓秽第一旨，
炎武语出尸子论；
商隐咏史警后世，

With weakened belief one will be out of mind,
How dare to he resist the disasters of every kind?
Only when one tries hard to keep him steadfast,
Can he resist any invasion of wickedness at last.

(Section XLI)

Throughout all the countries nowadays and old,
Their collapse by corruption can be usually told;
During the Kaiyuan Reign of the Tang Dynasty,
Emperor Tang Xuanzong was slack in prosperity;
He was carried far away by the imperial music,
And the artful joyousness made him fantastic;
His royal palace was shaking in drums beating,
And all souls were crazy in rhymes chanting;
He lost himself in such a luxurious dissipation,
That he found himself in an instant depression;
In proud abandonment of rampant declination,
He got his empire ruined in an awful rebellion;
If his evil desire dare to be divinely cleared,
How dare to the disastrous wars be declared?
Anti-corruption is of primary importance for us,
Among others, we'd keep virtuous quality plus;
To keep spiritually clean is the first principle,
As was stressed by Gu Yanwu and other people;
As is signed by Li Shangyin in *An Ode to History*,

乐天醒世莫长恨。
欲正我党正百官，
励精图治乃首任；
匡正祛邪祖美德，
清正清廉清明焜；
以道事民不可止，
以清为党荡秽根；
天下兴亡匹夫责，
君子为学惠世人；
登山临水羽扇香，
怀抱经野经国心；
竹杖芒鞋轻胜马，
济世安民负平生。
破岩之水源涓泾，
敝日之木起葱青；
忽于细微以致大，
禁微则易救未辛，
恩不忍诲义不割，
去事之后未然明；
不治已病治未病，
已乱未乱未当行；
源头治理防微渐，
防患未然灭芽萌；
温水煮蛙信念失，
妖平害处敕责躬；
事态之萌亦防范，

Together with Bai Juyi's warning against mysery.
The righteous CPC relies on her good members,
And sound politics must be away from slumbers;
Anti-evil campaigns should rely upon our virtue,
By this means our great course can but continue;
We should serve the people along the golden way,
Till all sinfulness has been get rid of for the Party;
We'd bear the responsibility for China to be better,
A true noble man should benefit the ones in tatter;
No matter where a true man is present, high or low,
He should maintain a for-people mission to follow;
Even if he is trapped into a plain and simple life,
He should break his way out for the national strife.
Water drops gathered can smash mountains steep,
And young plants grown can get their roots deep;
Something majestic is but derived from the tiny,
And it would be easy to settle the things initially,
It hard to punish ruthlessly the ones who are dear,
And one would be dizzy even things appear;
A disease in the earliest stage will be easily cured,
And the pre-time riot will be favorably secured;
Source management is needed from the beginning,
And disasters should be prevented at their rooting;
Slow dullness will make one slack in each action,
And anti-evil campaign needs all our participation;
We must be precautious of each troublesome issue,

范晔汉书赞丁鸿。

（第四十二节）

新型政商关系亲，
君子之交超然纯；
杜绝封建红顶商，
亲清两字为底蕴；
公私分明交有道，
廉洁互信敬如宾；
阅尽人间真情美，
共产党人如北辰。
人民利益是顶峰，
一切行动皆服从；
裙带关系乱党政，
切忌亲属借风型；
巴掌遮眼五指山，
切忌属地抱团型；
牢记人民大家庭，
切忌行业垄断型；
潜移默化成小径，
切忌秘书跟随型；
腐化堕落烂根芽，
根除商业进贡型；
政治利益结集团，
国家利益无影踪；

And historical wisdom can be used when it is due.

(Section XLII)

The new political-commercial relations are close,
In that a true man should have purity to suppose;
The two realms should not be feudally mingled,
And a clear distinction must for sure be burgled;
Public interests must be told from the private,
And honest trust can bring about due workmate;
Having experienced the true love of human beings.
The CPC will go for the people's well-being.
The people's interests are of the most importance,
For which we should do everything in obedience;
Relations-orientation will drive our work messy,
Therefore we must prevent from taking it easy;
Sometime a small interest will one near-sighted,
Thus we should stop the ill deeds dark-lighted;
We'd keep all the people as a big family in mind,
In all industries we'd ban monopoly of any kind;
Drops of water will unconsciously form a brook,
An official must not promote his men for a hook;
Degraded corruption will make us rot at bottom,
Profit dedication must be solved as a big problem;
Once the officials ganged for political pursuits,
They would for sure destroy the national interests;

疾亲民生无他念，
方能卓然志持恒；
霄汉高鸟瞰大地，
高峻如屏崤山冰。

Only if we go all out for the people's well-being,
Can we strive forward for better with time being;
As a hawk is flying high looking down at the earth,
Even the icy mountains are screened underneath.

第八章
Chapter Eight

敬民笃行篇

Ode to Hearty Respect for the People

（第四十三节）

铜古人镜为三鉴，
视水视民察下情：
以铜为鉴正衣冠，
以古为鉴知替兴，
以人为鉴明得失，
民情为镜替天行；
民情视为载舟水，
民情视为树之根，
民情视为种子地，
依靠民情为民情；
自说自话自谈唱，
节物风光不相从；
不接民气荒园径，
闭门造车脱民生；
成汤标准镜子论，
司马告诫细语声；
等闲识得东风面，
千家万户总是春。
心无百姓莫为官，
为官发财两道行；
心存百姓春浩浩，
丹心照破夜沉沉；
权力价值为公共，

(Section XLIII)

In our daily life three items are essential,
By self-discipline we'd work for people:
By mirror we can see if we're well-dressed,
By history we know how we are progressed,
By others' persuasion we know right or not,
And by the people we're righteous far a lot;
The people are the water to carry the boat,
And the people to the Party are as the root,
The people are to us what the land to seeds,
And we must serve them with all our deeds;
If we boast ourselves with dull empty words,
The people will despise us as the silly birds;
If we break away from the majority of mass,
We'll be trapped in mud like a desperate ass;
By self-discipline we'll become great sages,
As has been warned by Sima Qian for ages;
Only when we do keep ourselves righteous,
Can we supported by the people generous.
On official posts we must go for the people,
Official duty and profit cannot be a couple;
He for the people will be warmly admired,
Despite hardships he is unselfishly required;
All official power must be used for the public,

鞠躬尽瘁死后心；
但愿苍生俱饱暖，
不辞辛苦出山林。
莫嫌官小有大用，
常闻民间疾苦声；
春到民间草木知，
一枝一叶总关情；
吃穿百姓已百姓，
不欺百姓为官经；
干在实处走在前，
失官不辱得不荣。

（第四十四节）

政之所废逆民情，
政之所兴顺民心；
乐贵安育民四顺，
齐稷管仲著牧民；
百姓之意为我意，
民意所望细细闻；
共同富裕稳步进，
有梅有雪方精神。
治政之要于安民，
安民之要察疾情；
膏泽黎庶寰宇颂，
民心固结邦本宁；

And till death one will dedicate enthusiastic;
We wish that the mass be mutually wealthy,
For which all hardship for us will be worthy.
Even a petty official will contribute a lot,
Usually we'll behold if they are ill or not;
The grass knows first the arrival of spring,
As it acutely sense the world surrounding;
Being the people, we should rely on them,
And for them, we'll solve every problem;
We must take actions ahead of the people,
And do any thing for them as an example.

(Section XLIV)

Political corruption is making the people ill,
And right undertakings will meet their will;
We should let them live in peaceful comfort,
As was said by Guan Zhong on such a sort;
The people's demands are the same as mine,
And the people's appeals will be heard fine;
Let's go steadily for the common abundance,
Plumes against snow prove the right stance.
The core of politics is to let people peaceful,
And their peace depends on the sure dutiful;
Our goodwill to them can be highly chanted,
And the people's support would be counted;

若未察解民疾苦，
遑论民安谈民生；
根本利益属民众，
为着万千众民情；
悟得人民心中愿，
方能凝聚论复兴；
红雨随心翻作浪，
天连五岭飘旌缨；
敢与昆仑崩绝壁，
地动山摇鬼神惊。
天下之忧忧而忧，
天下之乐乐而民；
乐民之乐论发展，
忧民之忧体民衷；
天下之忧忧而先，
天下之乐乐后行；
百年风雨百年梦，
一以贯之持以恒；
人民镌刻旗帜上，
以德报德鱼水情。
高尚品德爱百姓，
宽厚行为百姓称，
低劣品德苛百姓，
卑贱行为百姓坑；
高尚低劣不合流，
宽厚卑贱泾渭明；

Without inspecting the people's difficulties,

How can we boast to care for their realities;

The basic interests belong to the great mass,

And for them we should make more progress;

If we keep the people's requirements in our mind,

We can unite together for the better of any kind;

Our sincere wish can bring about due showers,

Which will make our land rich with flowers;

We dare to smash the mountain of obstacles,

And we can shock the gods with spectacles.

We'll worry about the people when in danger,

And we'll be nice with whoever is a stranger;

To be nice to them we'll endeavor for future,

And to ease them we get chances to capture;

In face of any crisis we can go all out ahead,

And for comfort we follow the mass instead;

Last century found China in a dreamy storm,

And witnessed our struggles in the uniform;

On our flags was inscribed the people's will,

And our emotion will make the heaven thrill.

We have love for the folk with noble virtue,

And in return we earn their praise quite due,

If we treat the people in a degraded manner,

We'll stain the glories in the Party's banner;

The noble and the mean make a difference,

To keep righteous we hold fast perseverance;

晏子春秋书大义，
之江新语写心声；
莫让鱼水化油水，
莫让行贱害民生；
愿望稻菽千重浪，
愿享青山绿水情。

（第四十五节）

除患去疾解民痛，
腹心之疾症非轻；
百姓之疾腹心疾，
百姓疾苦必除清；
苏辙书呈皇帝书，
仿佛时时耳边声；
民安君卿安然睡，
未到晓钟享黎明。
日照大江东流奔，
民生紧系国运焜；
安得广厦千万座，
大庇天下寒士身；
细草微风潜入夜，
历久弥新济民心；
风雨不动安如山，
自身以苦护子莘；
闻其饥寒为之哀，

The Righteous was coded by Yanzi, the sage,
Which has been cited anew in Zhijiang's page;
Don't let intimation turn into awful corruption,
Nor let the evil-doers bring about humiliation;
Let there be a world prosperous and booming,
On the picturesque land we're merrily roaming.

(Section XLV)

The people must be relieved of great miseries,
Because this can be vital in national realities;
The people's hardship should be fully noticed,
And the comfort of them should be practiced;
Su Zhe once warned in the wicked old days,
His words have been retold even nowadays;
In time of peace the empire dare to lie in ease,
And the king with his men had a lot to please.
As water in the rivers flows down to the east,
A country's fate is related to the mass at least;
How can we have enough spacious buildings,
In which all noble scholars enjoy their livings;
Our cares to people is like gentle spring wind,
Which will benefit the people till the far end;
We shall keep firm in spite of varied changes,
In order to fight for people on the challenges;
We'll be sorrowful at their hunger and thirst,

见其穷苦心如焚；
纸船明烛冲天燃，
手握长缨泪倾盆；
愿为苍生取肝胆，
万里长空舞忠魂。
厉民之事毫末去，
利民之事丝发兴；
不以一己利为利，
而使天下利为公；
不以一己害为害，
而使天下释其轻；
事有利民厚其本，
事有利民深其根；
事有害民拔其本，
事有害民断其根；
最爱民众高唱至，
遍地桑麻物华吟。
功崇惟志志向远，
业广惟勤务实风；
料峭春风吹人醒，
东方欲晓催君行。

（第四十六节）

为人在世莫嗜懒，
百事由懒事不成；

To find their poverty we are burning at first;

Our sincere pray will prove nothing after all,

But rather we would gather in arms tearful;

For the people we would shed heroic blood,

And in every fiber let all our courage flood.

We never do anything harmful to the people,

And we'll do everything if it's duly suitable;

The private interests shall not be sought for,

But rather one would dedicate himself to all;

One should not worry about his own loss,

But keep in mind the good of the mass;

One would settle down whatever is favorable,

And deepen that which benefits the people;

And one must get rid of whatever is harmful,

And also eradicate all that is wicked and evil;

If we enchant that we for sure love the mass,

We should care for them and even their grass.

With great feats we shall achieve far more,

And by hard work we go steadily after all;

The spring wind will make our mind clear,

And at dawn we'll approach our goal near.

(Section XLVI)

We in the world must be hard-working,

Being lazy we shall accomplish nothing;

一勤天下无难事，
万里青云可致身。
合抱之木始毫末，
始于足下千里行；
九层之台起累土，
积土成山寸寸功；
锲而不舍凌云志，
经年累月杵成针。
大厦之巍非一木，
众流汇归大海润；
万丈高楼平地起，
中兴大业众谋成。
滴水穿石难于易，
绳锯木断大于星；
无易无难瑰丽梦，
无小无大一场空；
圣人源自庸人来，
庸人易小圣人成。
慎易避难远灾祸，
敬细远大微微功；
千里长堤溃蚁穴，
百尺之室隙焚红；
骐骥疾非一足力，
大鹏翔非一羽轻；
辉煌罗马始于无，
人类万世传文明。

We'll win everywhere if we're intelligent,
If we will we can succeed at any moment.
A high tree tends to grow from a tiny seed,
Any way dare to be covered at a low speed;
A lofty tower will be built from beneath,
And a mountain is made by piles of earth;
If we strive in perseverance with iron will,
We dare to wear a trunk into a thin needle.
A mansion can not be built by a single tree,
And many rivers gather into the very sea;
A towering mansion should be built abase,
And the great course be done pace by pace.
Even a rock can be holed by the water drop,
And a tree trunk can be sawed with a rope;
In reality there must be many a difficulty,
And without cordiality, life is but empty;
The sage comes from the common person,
And a man for bigger will become a Samson.
We should try hard to keep from disasters,
And it is no use if we're trapped in clusters;
A tiny mistake will bring about great losses,
And a spark will burn down rows of houses;
A single part can't make a whole machine,
And only a branch can't make trees in line;
The City of Rome can not be built in a day,
And humanity is passed century by century.

（第四十七节）

物有甘苦需共尝，
道有夷险需履行；
求实于名未见实，
观形于声未见形；
鞋子适脚自履知，
梨子亲尝甘味浓；
十三亿众登天道，
一路歌来一路情。
西门治邺察民生，
全功成名布义通；
耳闻目识手足践，
名闻天下泽后生；
脚上有泥心有数，
摸爬滚打需担承；
千磨万击坚意志，
百炼成钢万户崇。
不听虚言不浮术，
为民务实清廉风；
术必有典言有用，
不兴伪事不华名；
不学南朝谈虚务，
不学赵括纸上兵；
牡丹花好空入目，
名必有实事必功；

(Section XLVII)

The sweet and bitter we'd mutually share,

And the hardships we'd also together bear;

The reality cannot avail in vanity names,

And reputation will go bad by false fames;

The foot will know if the shoes are suitable,

By eating the pear can one know if eatable;

All China is going up on the righteous way,

We're marching on as songs heard far away.

As Ximen Bao governed the Yexian County,

For the people he was admirable for his duty;

On each fiber he got the sense of dedication,

And by duty he ran into a national reputation;

We should be aware of the post where we are,

In face of any challenges we overcome so far;

We should be of iron will against any torture,

By which we will be highly praised in future.

We should turn a deaf ear to the words empty,

But rather serve the people in actual honesty;

For our deeds we'll abide by sages' direction,

And we'll rid any vanity or artful decoration;

We'll not say big words like a historical figure,

Nor can we have things ruined in a fine gesture;

The peony isn't got as food despite its charm,

A good reputation should be practical in arm;

崇实充实先贤赐,
枣花虽小结实成;
空谈误国实兴邦,
荀悦申鉴警钟鸣。

The sages have bestowed us the golden rule,
And we dare to achieve a lot by this principle;
Empty talks will for certain ruin our country,
As has been warned in classics of our history.

第九章
Chapter Nine

育人任贤篇
Ode to Decent Education and Sound Official Appointment

（第四十八节）

苟新日新又日新，
澡雪浴德而洁心；
照镜正冠治未病，
品德修炼洗精神；
花儿无色吐清芬，
梅花抗寒迎新春；
普天万物太阳浴，
苏世独立固本心；
日新学子必日进，
日新月异又一村；
不日新者必自退，
不进则退步后尘；
今日广厦千千万，
万类霜天竞自骋；
学如逆水来行舟，
风吹浪卷励其身；
上天入地日不瞬，
谁主沉浮学为尊。
水积不厚难负舟，
风积不厚难负鹏；
鹏鸟高飞九万里，
背负青天乘雄风；
积蓄不深草作船，

(Section XLVIII)

For us tomorrow is for sure another day,
And on each day we'd go in a noble way;
We should keep ourselves fit beforehand,
Just as the divine angels in the holy land;
The fragrant flowers tend to be colorless,
And plumes can be blooming in coldness;
Everything is sun-bathed in outside world,
But every one must keep itself in the field;
A learner must make progress every day,
And he would achieve more without delay;
He'll fail one day if he ceases to take pace,
And without progress he'll lose his place;
Today we are met with many opportunities,
Against various challenges to face realities;
Learning is like rowing a boat up the river,
Among the tides one will struggle for ever;
No matter where it is we must take it easy,
No matter who we are we'd be of dignity.
A ship can't sail in shallow water,
And a frail camel can not go long to barter;
A strong swan can endure a far emigration,
And it can cover it duly before destination;
Without sure preparation one can't go afar,

基础扎牢方可成；
厚积薄发探骊珠，
雨露滋润成精英。
世情国情与党情，
时事变幻风云中；
新术不顶老术废，
硬术不敢软无能；
读书修身立品德，
传统精典必传承；
泱泱华夏五千年，
成长之梯贤铸成；
满园春色关不住，
东方荷花别样红。

（第四十九节）

此生有涯知无涯，
朝闻夕死乐其中；
时不我待勤为径，
浩然正气混天成。
含英咀华润年轮，
腹有诗书精自纯；
捧卷追贤养正气，
明智灵秀目含神；
周密深刻蕴庄重，
一鸟入林鸦无音。

And in firm basis one would be a great star;
In sure accumulation he'll be a big success,
Under due conditions he'll make progress.
Of the situations on our nation and Party,
We can trace something of the uncertainty;
The new course requires up-to-date skills,
Without which we'd lack workable wills;
We shall be perfect in learning and virtue,
And also must let the tradition to continue;
During five thousand years of our history,
Our sages have created a successful story;
Our charms will never be broken away,
As our wisdom can exist in a unique way.

(Section XLIX)

Knowledge is boundless in our limited life,
And we should try merrily for many a strife;
Time will await nobody but for intelligence,
Solemn nobility is of the most importance.
Virtuous wisdom makes us rich with grace,
And inner knowledge shows where to trace;
With classics we'll chase for righteousness,
And charming wisdom mirrors our acuteness;
By profound depth one can appear sublimity,
As a peacock can join crows in tranquility.

独上高楼天望尽,
志存高远耐清贫;
衣带渐宽终不悔,
孜孜不倦持之恒;
经年磨砚铁砚穿,
灯火阑珊笑意浓;
心坚志定穿日月,
不畏艰难登刃峰。
学不思罔终迷惑,
思不学殆徒劳神;
仲尼学琴重参悟,
怡然高望神色凝;
文王操曲如灵现,
襄子欣欣赞孺生;
善读史书勤思辨,
人云亦云亦无云。
知学不枉渡此生,
好学此生滋味浓;
乐而学学如美酒,
歌月舞影亦忘情;
望道蘸墨甜如粽,
吾醉长歌做先行;
痴痴呆呆咀宣言,
我辈方能识幽灵。

On the top of a high tower one can look afar,

And with noble aim we'll know who we are;

We would never repent with seas of tortures,

But work tirelessly as long–distance adventures;

With perseverance we'll even move the earth,

For only quite a few dare to embrace the truth;

With a firm will we can hold the world fast,

And we can get the decisive victory at last.

To learn without consideration can go astray,

And mere meditation is but waste of energy;

Confucius learned the music by inspiration,

In great pleasure he got the art imagination.

He saized the true spirit of Zhou Wenwang,

Which earned a praise from his tutor Xiang;

We'd read history classics in consideration,

And try to find the truth by self–meditation.

With true knowledge we'll live a life due,

And by hard work we'll enjoy quite a few;

Nothing is more pleasant than knowledge,

Which will carry us away in fanatic nudge;

Sometimes we would get lost in learning,

As the true knowledge is that interesting;

Once we read the Communist Manifesto,

We'll be inspired by Marxism in embryo.

（第五十节）

自古兴废系时序，
盛衰文变染世情；
唐尧兴盛击壤歌，
虞舜清明颂南风；
厉幽黑暗愤板荡，
时运交移质文形；
建安风骨盛唐象，
文心雕龙描世情；
今朝学子逢盛景，
时代风貌放歌声。
不积跬步无至远，
不积小流海难成；
心浮气躁浅辄止，
循序渐进圣言忠；
积善成德神明得，
积水成渊蛟龙生；
骐骥一跃不能十，
驽马十驾不舍功；
锲而不舍金石镂，
百年磨剑啸长空；
书山学海真遨游，
谆谆劝学若荀翁。
昨夜星辰昨夜风，
何事居穷道不穷；

(Section L)

Ancient time saw China booming or not,

And cultural feature would affect it a lot;

In time of Yao was heard *Ode to Farmers*,

And in that of Shun was *Ode to Summers*;

In reigns of Li and Yo in the early history,

Indignation dare to be heard in the country;

The Tang Dynasty dare to see poetry booming,

Ants of men of letters began mushrooming;

The present days witness a period majestic,

All the nation are rich with spirits fantastic.

Pace by pace one has a long distance to cover,

And a sea is formed with water from each river;

Being too restless one can not be a success,

By a due sequence one can make a progress;

With good virtues one can attain a top stage,

And by perseverance one has more to wage;

A good horse can't cover long at one stride,

But a slow one will run faraway with a ride;

In perseverance we will be second to none,

With no matches we have so far gone alone;

We shall feel free in pursuit for knowledge,

Which has been advised by Xunzi the sage.

Our life will be past like the wind yesterday,

But the Tao remains eternal even if all away;

少年辛苦终身事，
野泉声入砚池中；
悬梁刺股墨未干，
月斜楼上五更钟；
三十功名尘与土，
莫向光阴惰寸功。

（第五十一节）

凭贵或以贱为本，
处高或以下为根；
处下居后谦卑正，
根深叶茂求大成；
信息时代几何率，
知识更新换代频；
老化僵化思想钝，
难负授业载传承；
知识传递负使命，
传道解惑世尊崇；
庄子乐书逍遥游，
老子亦曾嘱后生；
师者应存海洋光，
甘洒雨露滋子莘。
独学无友孤陋闻，
时过后学苦难成；
察纳雅言金玉友，

Hard work at youth will benefit all our fate,
And the impulse to work is never too late;
Great pains should be taken to learn more,
Even overnight one can get a lot to explore;
Fames and feats are but vanity and nothing,
With time passed one should keep on working.

(Section LI)

To be noble one must settle down to earth,
To be aloft one will get rooted underneath;
Only when one behaves in a modest way,
Dare to he stand out without going astray;
Take nowadays geometry as an example,
The knowledge is changing quite multiple;
If one is slow-minded at the present time,
He will fail to fulfill his mission sublime;
We should convey the truth as our duty,
And take education course as a dignity;
As is recorded in the work by Zhuangzi,
And also in the doctrines given by Laozi;
A teacher should be knowledgeable like a sea,
And teach the young duly as he dare to be.
One can't be achievable when he is alone,
And if it is overdue he would obtain none;
One should from good friends take advice,

仲淹共读帐漆顶。
君子为学未必仕，
仕者为学方为君；
不学则愚学则智，
不学则乱学则兴；
盲人骑马迷失途，
夜半临池知惶恐；
少知而迷庸自扰，
不知而盲空余生。
学富五车须力践，
才高八斗融汇通；
心到眼到口到日，
少壮功夫老始成；
纸上得来终觉浅，
绝知此事要躬行；
陆翁冬夜示子书，
学子今晨座右铭。
广渊通达称博学，
详细周到审问清；
缜密思考堪慎思，
去伪存真需辨明；
剔粗取精分良莠，
一心一意即笃行；
蓬山此去无别路，
学以致用奔征程。

By which he would run into the fame nice.
A noble man mustn't be at an official post,
But an official should be learning at most;
A wise man without learning will be silly,
A society with knowledge will be orderly;
A blind man on a horse back will get lost,
And in ignorance we'll have much to cost;
With less knowledge one would turn banal,
And in blind ignorant one is but an animal.
To turn learned one should take great pains,
By this means one dare to obtain great gains;
At the very day when we keep all in detail,
We have accomplish our task true and real;
Knowledge on books is something empty,
Which is feasible when we turn it to reality;
Behold the poem by Lu You to his children,
Which can be treated as a motto by the men.
A true scholar will have seas of knowledge,
And in detail he would give a perfect nudge;
By careful thoughts he will have no faults,
And in exact manner he can get good results;
He dare to distinguish the good from the bad,
And as he does it attentively he is very glad;
There is no other way toward the top stage,
But rather one should go for it with courage.

（第五十二节）

才如箭镞学如弓，
闻鸡起舞贵有恒；
弓弩弯弯如满月，
箭镞疾疾似流星；
美矣梦想自学始，
勤奋青春远航冲；
一日之曝十日寒，
三更明月诵黎明。
学所益才以致用，
磨砺刃出剑锋铿；
梅花香自苦寒来，
采博多习胜孤行；
举目远眺非跂望，
臂不加长因高登；
鱼水鸟风草木时，
顺风而呼远应声；
窗竹影摇促膝论，
酒酣耳热国是争；
远山茅屋油灯闪，
晨曦吟啸龙虎行。
少年捧书似晨虹，
壮而好学如日中；
老而伏案如秉烛，
烛光闪闪彻夜明；

(Section LII)

Talent is like an arrow and learning a bow,
To study one must get a firm rule to follow;
When the bow is opened it is like the moon,
And the arrow on it will fly forward soon;
The dreamy ideal comes from the learning,
And glorious youth is related to dedicating;
Good effort can be exerted in a persistence,
And laziness should be got rid in resistance.
The true learning depends on actual usage,
There's a success when one dare to indulge;
Fragrance of plume flowers obtains in cold,
And to practice more one can't be too bold;
With good sight one look clearly far away,
And by going up one's hands are high to lay;
Like the fish in water and birds in the wind,
By observing we can tell each of their kind;
At window we can chat in face of bamboos,
And drinking liquor we'll talk about taboos;
Don't look down upon the distant log cabin,
Maybe there is a heroic young man living in.
The youth for knowledge is the fresh sun,
And the middle-aged is like that at noon;
And an aged learner is a walker by candle,
Which can make himself so easy to handle;

师旷盲翁天言示，
岂是儿戏晋平公？
之推家训犹在耳，
百年三读乐平生。

（第五十三节）

为政之要首在人，
见贤思齐蔚然风；
为人上者明如镜，
群下之能焯然形；
一贤立则群贤至，
从严治党治吏经。
书生君相起州部，
勇冠三军始卒功；
爵禄厚之而愈劝，
迁官袭级不恃功；
圣读显学韩非子，
百炼成钢铸精英。
非常之人非常功，
济济多士文王宁；
泛马趹弛严来教，
茂才异士堪大用；
马或奔踶致千里，
士或负俗立功名；
司马相如肝胆书，

As the blind man Shi Kuang once claimed,
Serious lessons can be occasionally aimed.
And behold the family doctrines by the Yan,
To observe it one may be as happy as one can.

(Section LIII)

Politics is related to the choice of officials,
Right men in right posts is of fundamentals;
If the senior officials are quite just and wise,
The junior ones will faithfully give service;
All are virtuous when the chief is in due line,
And a righteous party relies on due discipline.
Some princes and ministers ascended lower,
And with bravery they began come to power;
With great honor they would endeavor more,
But not boast their feats or high post after all;
One should learn from *Hanfeizi* to be a sage,
And true hero will be throughout a long age.
The unique person can create the unique feats,
And the sage king is at ease with many talents;
By strict training a banal horse can be excellent,
And great mission is for a man with high talent;
A horse with a whip can cover a long distance,
And a noble man will be famous at due stance;
Once Sima Xiangru wrote a fine poetic prose,

汉武将才兹为盛；
神八太空吻玉兔，
天公月球步闲庭；
而今惜才堪比古，
九州生气恃雷风；
我劝天公重抖擞，
不拘一格降俊英。
由得人也邦之兴，
由失人也邦之终；
得其人也失其人，
然非一朝一日凭；
雷峰塔倒轰然间，
亦非一朝一日倾；
天地不能顿寒暑，
渐于春秋至夏冬；
社稷不会瞬兴亡，
渐于善恶论亡兴；
不任贤才国空虚，
不用良士国无政；
兴亡之由策林辩，
香山居士嘱聆听；
积善之庙信者众，
积贤之堂年年丰。

With the praise by Emperor Hanwudi he rose;

When *Shenzhou* 8 roams in the space,

Like an angel it was idling on moon surface;

Now China needs more talents than before,

The old nation are earnest for talents more;

I do wish heaven bless our lovable country,

By giving us any able men in each century.

With the talents our nation will be booming,

And with none we'll doom to be declining;

But talents can't be obtained by short term,

We shall gradually by education get them;

A tower will collapse down in a moment,

But for a long time it has some movement;

The winter to summer can't turn too fast,

The four seasons must be in circle at last;

A nation will not boom or incline quickly,

With corruption it will move down evilly;

By bad appointment a nation will weaken,

And the political crisis will surly deepen;

The national fate has long been discussed,

And there're many wise men being fussed;

A temple with good will dare to be the best,

And a count with talents endures any test.

（第五十四节）

千羊之皮一狐腋，
狐腋之昂似貂绒；
千人诺诺比花朵，
一士谔谔金石声；
良药苦口利于病，
忠言逆耳利于行；
赵良忠言比药石，
司马煎药苦后生。
不知人长不知用，
不知人短不妄评；
应知长中亦有短，
应知人短寓长中；
用人之长辟之短，
去短用长慧眼清；
仅用己近用己明，
远祸隐然藏短中；
先贤魏源修默觚，
今贤用人应辩通。
骏马历险不能耕，
田牛虽壮难驰骋；
坚车载重不渡河，
偏舟履水疾如风；
寸有所长尺有短，
舍长就短难以行；

(Section LIV)

A thousand pieces of sheep fur cost far less,
Than a piece of fox skin which is priceless;
Thousands men's gossip is but enchanting,
But advice by a noble man is enlightening;
Bitter medicines will be of curable effect,
And cordial words sounds not all the best;
Zhao Liang once took criticism as the drug,
And it is said a criticism-hater is but a bug.
One can be posted if knowing he's virtuous,
In saying of others one should keep cautious;
No one in the world is all right and no wrong,
And it's no use disputing if it's short or long;
A wise leader will choose his men by talent,
By clear direction he will avail management;
If the leader just relies on his own wisdom,
There in the work will arouse a big problem;
Wei Yuan said that one should keep silent,
Which should be wisely adopted at present.
As a war horse can not be used in the land,
And an ox will be uneasy in a wrong band;
A heavily-loaded cart will not cross a river,
And a boat with wind goes faster than ever;
Everyone has the merits and shortcomings,
Nothing dare to go beyond its surroundings;

生材贵适勿苛求，
用长用短君眼明；
智者为谋知短长，
至简至理寓杂兴。
文王多士周朝生，
赖以重士维国祯；
济济多士国事盛，
礼贤尊士得人心；
大风起兮云飞鸿，
威加海内故乡名；
精心栽育梧桐树，
引得凰来凤开屏；
治国安邦求良才，
安得猛士功勋戎。

The suitable one will prove to be the best,
How to use it one can use his eyes to test;
A wise leader should know what is right,
And the simple methods would be bright.
The Zhou was booming with many a talent,
With whom the dynasty saw a development;
Plenty of talents make a country prosperous,
As the leaders are but modesty and virtuous;
In the big wind a swan dare to fly more loftily,
And by big feats a man will be famous easily;
If preparations have been done before hand,
Talents will be called on here in a big band;
Great talents are needed in the political stage,
And soldiers are wanted with a war to wage.

第十章
Chapter Ten

战略思维篇
Ode to Strategic Thinking

（第五十五节）

中国核心价值观，
二十四字玉其成：
倡导富强与民主，
文明和谐理念凝，
倡导自由与平等，
公正法治大国风，
倡导爱国与敬业，
诚信友善君准绳；
二十四字字字金，
国民信仰筑心灵；
人间屋屋声朗朗，
桑梓处处山青青。
战略清醒目炯炯，
战略定力如卧钟；
大国对比靠实力，
赢得未来赢主动；
洞察判断大决策，
果敢坚定来执行；
回首叫云飞风起，
浪花淘尽显英雄。
战略思维大胸襟，
历史思维知古今，
辩证思维哲思辨，

(Section LV)

Behold the core values of the Chinese people,
Which in concise terms serve as a good example:
Strength and democracy are promoted so highly,
Along with the ideas of civilization and harmony,
We also have freedom and equality to highlight,
And a government of justice and law in our sight,
Stressed are patriotism and professional loyalty,
Together with criteria of friendship and cordiality;
The twenty-four Chinese characters are like gold,
Which dare to forge the hearts of us, young and old;
The doctrines have been heard in each household,
And also in every village among hills been told.
With strategic sight we will keep a clear mind,
And stand steadily for challenges of every kind;
By actual power we can match other powers big,
As for the core interest there is no leaves of fig;
Big decisions should be done by sound judgment,
Before all of us go firmly forward to implement;
Like a fit of wind we can whirl clouds in the sky,
When sand is gone, the gold is seen where to lie.
The strategic thinking shows the high conception,
The historical thoughts illustrate vast perception,
Dialectical thinking has a philosophy dimension,

创新思维破旧陈,
底线思维时忧患,
居安思危存乎心;
日暖桑麻光似泼,
丹枫静若玉麒麟。

(第五十六节)

古曰五行无常胜,
兵无常势水无形;
又曰四时无常位,
日有短长月死生;
因地制水高低流,
避实击虚克敌赢;
孙武用兵无常态,
春秋虚实无恒形;
刚愎自用盲动症,
蔑视辩证受以惩;
抱残守缺茧自缚,
恩哲至赞辩证型;
东西大哲滔滔著,
称得人间圣哲公;
今朝改革大门敞,
任何事物需辩证;
前人哲思我乘凉,
梦里敢不谢仙翁?

And original ideas possess the breaking tension,

Bottom-line notion means anxiety for the future,

And worrying in peace is something of mixture;

As the blazing sun is bathing our hometown,

Maples stand still with leaves up and down.

(Section LVI)

Our ancestors said there is no constant victory,

And the same thing happens on actions military;

It was also said the seasons have some alteration,

The days are changing with the earth's rotation;

Ground patterns make water downward flow,

And the military arts are used to defeat the foe;

As Sun Wu the great military artist once did,

He has brought about a military science indeed;

If a commander wage a war in blind arrogance,

He would be punished because of his ignorance;

If he keeps hard to the out-dated waste doctrines,

He would be trapped in the dialectical disciplines;

As Engels once praised the works philosophical,

He is for sure called the dialectical master at all;

Nowadays the door of reform is widely opened,

And the dialectic thinking should be strengthened;

The former philosophic wisdom will benefit us,

To the masters we have gratitude for them to pass.

中国巨轮劈浪进，
高歌向前惊风云；
惊涛骇浪百舸争，
平流无石莫轻心；
泰坦尼克歌生平，
冰山至前一瞬瞠；
泾溪不险人兢慎，
终岁不闻倾覆人；
遇险不惊风帆顺，
亦因险恶能聚神；
乐极生悲漠无险，
时时闻说有沉沦；
杜荀鹤公描泾溪，
溪溪点悟后来君。
政令多繁不稳定，
保持定力稳步行；
才高心细治大国，
万变不能离其宗：
固守本根应万变，
多言数穷易守中。

（第五十七节）

改革必然百事生，
乱云飞渡应从容；
莫言改革即得利，

The ship of China is matching forward at a high speed,

With high enchantment it will be amazing indeed;

In furious waves many a ship goes for the contest,

Even in smoothness we'll steer our ship the best;

Behold the great legend of the well-known Titanic,

At the iceberg her glory turn to be awfully tragic;

Even on a flat way one should walk very carefully,

By this means one dare to get his journey peacefully;

One should not get terrified in face of any crisis,

But rather keep him as decently tranquil as he is;

Tragedies sometimes come from extreme gladness,

And a wreckage will be encountered in quietness;

Pay attention to the river pictures by Du Xunher,

We would be inspired by the ideas of the author.

Multiple political orders make the nation unstable,

Maintenance of steadiness proves a rule feasible;

A big country can be governed with fine talent,

Of any alteration we can come for development:

We should keep ourselves for various changes,

By talking less and acting more in the new ages.

(Section LVII)

In time of reform there must be varied problems,

With great ease we would settle down all items;

Do not say we promote reform merely for profit,

赚满盆钵数钱声；
正入金钱圈子里，
一笔获得一笔横；
上山容易下岭险，
切莫空欢抵山岭；
新的历史新特点，
遇事不慌握主动；
矛盾问题不避掩，
有备无患不懈松；
美金裹秽流中国，
底线思维心中明；
一年一度改革劲，
峥嵘岁月愈峥嵘。
能视百步不能睫，
大道难求因目轻；
碧山终日思不尽，
一叶障目神不清；
朝思暮想眼前事，
莫争旁骛自清醒；
张公千诗轻万家，
何以贡举怨终生？
真才实学不念它，
悉自优长莫恨公；
干好主业大道正，
山山池州登九峰。

And everyone is indulged in the material benefit;
If we lose ourselves in awful trap of the money,
We would be dragged into an ominous journey;
Going up is easy but going down is dangerous,
A slight slipping will prove our life disastrous;
The new era possesses the new characteristics,
And we should keep us tranquil in our politics;
We shall never steer away the contradiction,
But try hard to solve them in sure preparation;
Dollars have carry lots of dirt into our country,
With bottom thought we must sense the reality;
Year in year out we are marching for reform,
And we are met harsh challenges of any form.
We should look afar with a sound, acute sight,
By which to arrive at our destination bright;
One can think about various hills in his mind,
But a leaf on his eyes he cannot tell each kind;
We can encounter various matters everyday,
And we should hold them fast in a clear way;
Mr. Zhang was widely famous for his poems,
But for empty fame he finally lost his aims!
True learning has nothing to do with big fame,
And practical undertaking will bring fine name;
Only when we succeed in our general course,
We would enjoy our achievements of course.

（第五十八节）

一叶蔽目不见泰，
两豆塞耳不闻霆；
井底之蛙不言海，
夏虫笃时不认冰；
见画一色不知美，
见骥一毛不知腾；
井中视星不过数，
暗于大理难宏控；
峰顶观云五洲顾，
四海风云装我胸；
大计小事同此理，
绿茵场上理亦同：
马拉多纳我最爱，
球王浪得不虚名；
独立大队单兵进，
痛失神杯我心疼。
豪华战车日耳曼，
将帅合力马难行，
大力女神寓哲思，
团队合作功告成。
观察事物如游山，
各有高低各有峰；
多族之国美利坚，
华夏民族中国情；

(Section LVIII)

A leaf can block our sight toward world outside,
Two beans in our ears will deafen us from thunder;
A frog living in a well knows none about the sea,
And a bug living in the summer feels nothing icy;
One single color can not make a picture attractive,
Seeing only a part one can't get the comprehensive,
Only a few stars can reflect in the water of a well,
And without ultimate truth one has nothing to tell;
On top of a hill one can see the whole world clear,
All wind whistles dare to be heard in an acute ear;
There is the same law in any corner of the society,
So is that of soccer sports with fantastic specialty;
My beloved soccer star is distinguished Maradona,
He is most famous in the world as well as in China;
He tends to play independently along with his team,
It's a pity that single-handedness proves a shame;
The German soccer team is like a delicate machine,
With one heart and will they would play to win,
There exist some lessons in such sports and games,
Only by cooperation the team dare to run to fames.
When observing things we are like in a journey,
And different persons will find different scenery;
Compared with the multi-ethnic United States,
China is a unique big country with special traits;

若识庐山真面目，
跳出三界五行中；
失去自我不知云，
妄自菲薄盲目崇；
视野开阔凝目聚，
哈姆雷特台上行：
花开千朵各自赏，
王子各自心目中；
庐山或有仙人洞，
无限风光在险峰。

（第五十九节）

不谋万事不一时，
不谋全局不一城；
有容固先振其纲，
徐徐措节目之清；
登泰山而小天下，
功成无我天下胸；
洞幽烛微了于心，
见微知著腹藏兵；
闭目塞听封固步，
只见树木不见森；
战略思维握大事，
踏遍青山郁葱葱。
大局意识是关键，

If one want to possess a true understanding of it,
He must break away the prejudice of every bit;
Being trapped in ignorance one will turn blind,
With too much pride one is for sure out of mind;
With a wide vision we can watch more clearly,
As on the stage Hamlet learns to observe acutely:
Maybe there are various patterns of great beauties,
But the princes will not love the same in realities;
If you go to Lushan Mountain for Xianren Cave,
You'll see the dangerous parts can make us crave.

(Section LIX)

A wise leader should conceive most profoundly,
Rather than be trapped in messy issues aimlessly;
To make the principle firm is of most importance,
And everything will be kept in an orderly stance;
On a high position one will become more humble,
For in the nation he will prove to be respectable;
By heart the wise leader should trace everything,
By detail he will obtain the power earth-shaking;
If one stops going for better in self-satisfaction,
By prejudice he will gradually go to declination;
In strategic thinking he should grasp the principal,
Wherever he goes he should set a shining example.
Looking at the big picture is vital,

政治意识是本根，
看齐意识是条件，
核心意识是保证；
为谋山河添锦绣，
五风十雨惠无穷；
中国特色七彩图，
天悬明月独豪情。

And the political awareness affects us all,

The alignment awareness serves as the precondition,

And the leadership of the core is our foundation;

To make our country more and more beautiful,

We shall deliver our dedication more plentiful;

The Chinese characteristics are most magnificent,

In the sole joy we will enjoy victories complacent.

第十一章
Chapter Eleven

新时代篇
Ode to New Era

（第六十节）

创造小康目标准，
人民利益为中心；
调动民众积极性，
主动创造绣程锦；
人民利益高无尚，
共同富裕步步稳；
黄河九十九湾尽，
风驰呼啸奔海滨。
全民小康目标近，
全民健康乃根本；
为民康健造福祉，
健康中国种兰因；
遍地华佗虫无影，
绿水青山无瘟神。
高山流水绿又青，
金山银山灿又晶；
青山绿水是源泉，
绿色银行裕后生；
银山金山待发展，
不以增长论英雄；
青山不老绿水流，
金山银山砌长城。

(Section LX)

Our aim is the comprehensive well-off,

With the people's interests as the centre;

We should stimulate the people's vitalities,

To create a new world in the future;

The people's interests are of top importance,

For common prosperity we'll take the steady pace;

Behold the Yellow River flowing eastwards,

And crossing the land with so many zigzags.

The goal of overall wealth is coming near,

And the core of the people's health is clear;

The people's health is where happiness lies,

And a healthy nation is what Heaven supplies;

With good doctors around diseases are gone,

A healthy society is beautifully coming along.

Living among the green hills and beside clean water,

Our wealthy life is of the Chinese character;

Green mounts and clear rivers as our source,

Will bring about green banks for our course;

We've more allowances for our development,

And GDP index proves not so important;

With mountains fresh and rivers flowing long,

With our prosperity we will for sure go along.

（第六十一节）

经济发展新常态，
发展建设惠民生；
产业主体需转换，
创新成为新驱动；
硬骨难啃涉险滩，
历史辩证识特征；
直登云麓三千丈，
祺雾飘绕乐升平。
创新引领第一动，
人才资源第一撑；
理论制度科技文，
形成社会蔚然风；
天下清明无寒士，
霍然千丈翠岩屏。
大众创业始草根，
万众创新弄潮儿；
促进流动寓诚信，
创造价值量自身；
总理宏论达沃斯，
精神追求振国民；
富民之道强国策，
笑时犹带梅花嗔。
互联网+奇妙想，
传统行业双翅生；

(Section LXI)

Economic development is our new normalcy,

Which can benefit the people by the policy;

The industrial pillars should be transformed,

And innovation is the motive to be performed;

Whenever there have appeared the dangers,

We'll apply historical dialectics as triggers;

As we are ascending a high mountain foggy,

We'll be afresh with recovery of our energy.

We'll led the innovation as the locomotive,

The human resources make our course active;

By theoretical and scientific research systems,

We in our society can solve various problems;

Each talent will exert his effort to full degree,

A sound society will emerge as one can see.

Each ordinary person can be an entrepreneur,

And every one can show himself in the career;

By loyalty we shall stimulate the movement,

And actively we create more at each moment;

As Premier Li Keqiang once said at Davos,

The spiritua pursuit will conquer all woes;

Talking about the ways to make us strong,

He expressed excitement in a struggle long.

Together with internet and fancy thinking,

Carriers of old industries come into being;

乘法效应前瞻性,
促进绿色有效能;
网络传统双拥抱,
生态产业获激情;
彩索身轻长趁燕,
乐享其中不闻莺。
宏伟战略大数据,
三关四合大工程;
红日白浪望金山,
此乃悠悠万世功。
资源再生重利用,
分享经济新招兴;
以租代买乃本质,
两权分离资源丰;
新时代人新气象,
杨花任性倚东风。

（第六十二节）

二零二五新纲领,
中国制造穿石功;
十年磨剑刃如叶;
它日华山再论锋。
工匠精神塑自尊,
生生不息源泉根;
中国制造转创造,

To foresee this, one can develop multiply,

And green industries will rise effectively;

If we embrace the internet and tradition,

Ecological industry will arise in passion;

With this we dare to do more for integrity,

Till we've indulged ourselves in prosperity.

Big data will be used for our main strategies,

Great projects will be undertaken nowadays;

Great health will be created from nowhere,

This would become the wealth bank to share.

The renewable resources can be used again,

And it is the new approach for us to obtain;

It is essential to hire instead of purchase,

By dividing powers the capital does increase;

The people in the new era show a new look,

By free will we can try anything out of book.

(Section LXII)

2025 Program proves to be something new,

MADE IN CHINA has caught me and you;

A sharp sword is due to long-time grinding,

With it a true hero dare to be easily winning.

The spirit of craftsmanship is highly valued,

For many generations it has continued;

China is turning from imitation to creation,

中国速度转质品；
中国产品转品牌，
由量转质日日浸；
技术整合精求精，
曲无终曲永追寻。
构建新型城镇化，
崭新理念为引领；
四化三农亦注重，
农耕文明要传承；
滂然遥接现代化，
农业工业连环动；
夫行此去遵何路？
互联网+九州城！
志合不以山海远，
网络空间命运同；
深化合作共构建，
扩大共识互沟通；
互联网乃双刃剑，
宝库魔盒决水平；
推动全球新变革，
造福人类求共赢。
精准扶贫建机制，
帮助到位贫困人；
打赢脱贫攻坚战，
实效检验不含混；
青山着意滋万家，

And China's speed means a popular fashion;
China's goods become those of good brand,
The quality is going daily for a higher band;
All is for the better in technological integrity,
In endless efforts we're going with dignity.
On the way is the new urbanization,
Which is directed by the fresh conception;
Agricultural issues must be kept in mind,
And agri-civilization may not decline;
Agriculture must be modernized someday,
Which should come abreast with industry;
By which road can we get the destination?
It's the internet plus national organization!
Comrades come regardless the far distance,
The internet space has the same existence;
Cooperation should be deepened totally,
Common sense, too, expanded mutually;
The internet serves as a double-edged sword,
Well or ill, it will become a human lord;
Let us stimulate the new global reform,
Which can make Man happy in any norm.
The fine poverty-aid system must be run,
Since anti-poverty campaign has begun;
We must win the hard war against poverty,
And people's content means a true victory;
The families will live fine in the green hills ,

杨柳春风传福音。
海绵城市概念新,
适应环境弹性城;
积存渗透自净化,
人与自然和谐中;
枫径鸟啼盘空翎,
静听铜壶滴漏声。

(第六十三节)

负面清单需管理,
国际规则亦通行;
单外领域予开放,
各类主体皆平等。
自我革命放管服,
放权市场百姓声;
优化放管简当头,
深刻变革全身行;
背水一战大决心,
大道至简智慧功。
汉开中功名万里,
秋风细雨阵阵轻。
改革供给结构性,
实现整体高水平;
辩证结构供给侧,
互为条件相依存;

With charming scenery all bear holy wills.
Sponge city is of a newly-brand conception,
It refers to flexibility in urban construction;
It serves as a unity with a self-purified organ
In which Nature is in harmony with the Man;
In that the birds chirping in the ample road,
Where people live with the tranquil mood.

(Section LXIII)

The negative lists must be put under control,
For which we can use the rules international;
The bill-beyond areas can be legally opened,
And subjects of various kinds may be evened.
The leaders should behave by self-discipline,
And the mass will for sure be kept in due line;
Administration is carried away by simplicity,
Profound reform will go on with complicity;
We should be determined for a final battle,
Even the earth can be moved little by little;
He who benefit the people will be memorized,
Even a tiny deed will be gently popularized.
The supply structure should be reformed,
And the high level should entirely formed;
The dialectical structure comes by the side,
Which co-exist as inter-condition to provide;

相互配合协调进，
社会主义之根本；
日暮云合喷薄雾，
朝霞雾去旭日焞。
三去一降一补法，
优化适应性能灵；
产能过剩压力大，
严格控制量徒增；
经济管理大课题，
与日俱进步步营；
天马凤凰春香漫，
山川浩歌响赢钟。
国需改革促进派，
思想领先敦君行；
想改谋改善改革，
勇于改革重任承；
风清气正好环境，
整顿吏治正党风；
患得患失羽别姬，
落得无颜回江东。

（第六十四节）

中国方案任驰骋，
国际舞台舞纵横；
致力开辟新天地，

Each industry should be run in coordination,

Which is the core of the socialist dimension;

As it would be cloudy or fogy at the sunset,

While at dawn we can see a red sun beget.

We should adjust by increase or decrease,

And by nimble means we dare to do at ease;

Overcapacity is a big challenge,

And we should try our best to manage;

Economic governance is a general topic,

Day by day we shall undertake it strategic;

Take the horse and peacock as an example,

In sense of value both are uniquely ample.

Reform stimulators are needed at present,

Who should be of thoughtful advancement;

He should be good at reforming if he will,

And bear responsibility in a volunteer will;

At the environment with decent morality,

It is needed to for the cadres and the Party;

If the leaders think too much of his gains,

He would awfully fail by losing his last bits.

(Section LXIV)

The Chinese Program is of wild attraction,

which has earned international admiration;

With the program we'll open a new world,

国际减贫助进程；
气候治理全球动，
点亮世界互联灯；
中国信心网传递，
中国智慧闪星空。
总体国家安全观，
政治安全为准绳；
五大要素五关系，
建设持久与和平；
民人为本求发展，
和谐世界共繁荣；
舞榭歌台总风流，
千古江山泼丹青。
新的时代新思维，
合作共赢为核心；
结伴而行不结盟，
丛林法则要除根；
传统关系渐淡去，
新的世界要互尊；
绿色低碳可持续，
人与自然和谐亲；
万里烟浪云帆挂，
云海相搂群仙吟。

And international poverty can lessen wild;
We have launched climate governance,
By this means to enlighten all on the earth;
The Chinese confidence can be widespread,
And the Chinese wisdom can also be read.
Of the holistic view of the national security,
Political security should be of a top priority;
There are five elements and five relations,
All are for construction of secure nations;
We'll develop with the people as the basis,
And let the wild world be a booming oasis;
Worldly life can witness the world realistic,
But natural land looks always picturesque.
The new era will require the new thinking,
And the core of it lies in common winning;
We can walk together but not as an alliance,
The forest rule must be rid without trace;
The traditional relations are gradually away,
We'll live anew together in a respectful way;
The green and low-carbon life is sustainable,
Man and Nature are harmoniously amiable;
Let's go like a light boat sailed in the wind,
On a dreamy land with immortals behind.

（第六十五节）

新型大国关系重，
远近文明各不同；
总览世界大趋势，
人类皆亲诚惠容。
中俄关系率先领，
不结同盟不联盟，
相辅相成互支持，
相互补充不制衡。
中美关系至关重，
海洋两岸话太平。
习奥庄园达共识，
不急不抗不纷争；
卅年改革寻樵径，
发展互利皆为朋；
中美互礼互沟通，
皆愿世界大和平；
海湖会晤茶友好，
故宫外交品和茗；
四高对话常交流，
太平洋阔中美容。
中国智慧寓平等，
注入活水天下兴；
和平之父加尔通，
称赞中华大道行。

(Section LXV)

New relations of big countries count for much,

In that their civilizations are beyond a touch;

To look totally at the general world tendency,

All the human beings are apt to get intimacy.

The Sino-Russia relationship has gone ahead,

Being not alliances the two co-live instead,

Both the nations support and assist mutually,

And are related closely and complementally.

The Sino-US relations is of top importance,

Across the Pacific they affect world peace:

Xi Jinping and Obama have reached an agreement,

No conflicts arise to the other government;

For forty years we are hunting for a path,

By which the dispute can be set to earth;

China and the United States exchanged greetings,

Wishing for peace of global surroundings;

Leaders met at the lake as the tea mates,

And the Palace Museum saw their tea plates;

Bilateral dialogues have become common,

The Pacific hopes to witness the tolerant relation.

The Chinese wisdom refers to equality,

By living spirit it can bring all prosperity;

Galtung is labeled as the Father of Peace,

And he praises China for the Tao practice.

中西当今两气场，
两大气场两文明；
容下各异多样化，
国际民主大背景。
远亲不同各自好，
以邻结伴万事兴；
家门太平方安稳，
亲诚惠容四字经；
起望衣冠神州路，
太平洋上歌太平。

（第六十六节）

全球治理天道行，
共建共商共享羹。
人类命运共同体，
皆愿祥和与安宁；
呼唤文明放异彩，
相得益彰和谐生；
不输入出不复制，
中国模式自身挺；
友直友谅友多闻，
不辞辛劳维和平；
他山之石可攻玉，
交流互鉴多姿丰；
初始如一共产党，

China and West form two fields of energy,

And their cultures are of different integrity;

We should endure each other's diversity,

Under the main background of democracy.

We each have our own favorable traits,

Good neighbors will become kin mates;

National security will let us live at ease,

And goodwill can let neighbors to please;

With the overall national security present,

Over the Pacific can hear the enchantment.

(Section LXVI)

The globe should be governed in Holy Tao,

With co-efforts the rights are shared by all.

As to the community of the human destiny,

Luck and peace will be given to the many;

The colorful civilizations are appealed,

In diverse harmony our calamity is healed;

Without putting in or out, nor imitation,

The Chinese model is of robust representation.

The true fiends will be frank and faithful,

And they try to maintain peace after all;

We can mirror others valuable experience,

And co-exchange will bring convenience;

The goal of CPC was set in the beginning,

永为人类放鸽声。
亚信峰会阐宗旨，
开放经济求共赢；
忆逝往者不可谏，
来者可追共心同；
面临深刻四转变，
三期叠加不容轻；
谋求创新增长极，
挖掘发展新功能；
时代潮流不可逆，
双向经济互联动；
全球经济遇逆风，
唯有发展阔包容；
手把红旗旗不湿，
勇立潮头飓风迎；
百尺竿头须进步，
十方世界是全身；
东西开放新格局，
亚太板块大引擎；
人类命运共美好，
中国之梦相辉映；
理想虽遥不言弃，
东方西方共繁荣。
一跃冲天遨吴刚，
鸿鹄之志赢人心；
壮志放游云中酒，

She will bring peace forever as time being.

She showed herself in Asia-Pacific Summit,

By opening economy for wining bit by bit;

The past lessons have been gone for ever,

And coming chances belong to the mover;

In face of the profound Four Transforms,

We'll be aware of the unity of three forms;

For more growth we'll hunt for innovation,

And try to dig deeper for the new function;

The tide of the times will not go up the stream,

And bilateral economy will be of a co-team;

The global economy is developed adversely,

Only in expansion can it dig out desperately;

The breakthrough needs a leader of top wit,

By going ahead he'll draw the cart out of pit;

He'll be marching on from victory to victory,

For all the people he'll make a different history;

It is new that both the east and west are open,

Which will stimulate the Asia-Pacific region;

The human destiny is all the same wonderful,

And the Chinese dream will prove colorful,

We'll not abandon our ideal though faraway,

East and West will mutually prosper one day.

When *Shenzhou* was launched to the space,

China has earned applauds for her great pace;

When we drank for more in bold intention,

诸国群神乐纷纷；
车树云旗随风舞，
团团精气荡青云。
两岸同胞一家亲，
血浓于水乃天情；
求同存异纳百川，
五项原则话和平；
九二共识坚冰破，
守望相助亦三通；
时代命题君必作，
时代潮流君必行；
亲人团聚民福祉，
两岸统一天道行。

Which has stirred merry gods of each region;
Along with the banners flowing in the wind,
Our spirit are high as we are all determined.
The cross-Strait people are but one family,
Who prove to be blood-relatives naturally;
If varied unanimity can be mutually endured,
And with the Five Principles peace is secured;
By 1992 Consensus we will break the hard ice,
And we'll have a cross-Strait access by aid nice;
The mission has by the times been bestowed,
Along the trend no hesitation can be allowed;
No blessings are greater than family reunion,
And surely natural is the cross-strait unification.

尾声
Epilogue

敢当篇
Ode to the Willing Duties

（第六十七节）

向未来继续前进，
向前奔不忘初心；
宇宙精神胸中藏，
腾笼换鸟百舸奔。
无数民族无踪影，
皆因无有民族魂；
五千年史寓属性，
植根血脉传基因；
民胞物与和万邦，
中华文化地生根；
再注马列新理念，
指引共产主义真；
人民选择共产党，
大业千秋定乾坤；
中国版本我独有，
民族文化塑金身；
共产主义大目标，
中国特色绣程锦；
国富民强指日近，
再跨征鞍蹄扬尘；
率领百姓臻美景，
天之骄子系党魂；
新时代赋新思想，

(Section LXVII)

Let us go on marching toward the future,

And hold fast our initial ideal when mature;

Let the universal spirit hidden in our mind,

In a fresh life we throw the old days behind.

Many a nation has disappeared in reality,

As they lack the soul of their own identity;

Our quality is about five thousand years long,

And the unique gene has been handed down;

From the beginning we are innately peaceful,

And the Chinese culture makes us plentiful;

There input the new conceptions of Marxism,

Which will bring China up to Communism;

It is the people who have chosen the Party,

And this great choice has made history;

The Chinese feature is of sole originality,

Which comes rightly from the nationality;

Communism serves as the grand coming goal,

The Chinese feature of which is very typical;

The booming Chinese nation is near at hand,

We should work for better in our motherland;

Leading the people toward fine tomorrow,

President Xi points a route for us to follow;

A new thought is bestowed in the new era,

荣膺使命为人民；
天地翻覆执牛耳，
风起绿洲麦浪金；
二〇五〇品美酒，
牧童遥指地球村。

（第六十八节）

七十年披荆斩棘，
七十年风雨征程；
历史不能再选择，
把握现实追筑梦；
开创未来无反顾，
儿女圆梦宇宙腾；
众望所归膺众望，
道远任重铁肩承；
赠君一碗高粱酒，
以壮胆色青纱行：
敢登宇宙太空游，
九州儿女志成城；
敢把长江当匹练，
奔涛骇浪任驰骋；
敢持黄河长空舞，
信手舒卷捋东风；
敢叫日月供调遣，
风叱云咤履群峰；

For the people we've the mission to declare;

He can usher in the earth-shaking changes,

For a long age he's overcome many challenges;

At 2050 China will heel for her great booming,

Even a cowboy knows what China is meaning.

(Section LXVIII)

Seventy years has encountered hard struggles,

And seventy years has heard marching bugles;

History would present us no alternative choice,

And we'd hold ourselves at the dreamy voice;

The future will find all of us the creators dutiful,

As our dream coming true is universally cheerful;

With full expectation of the Chinese people,

We should go dutifully with courage ample;

Let me present you a cup of sorghum liquor,

To strengthen the courage to further conquer:

We dare to go deeper into the universe vast,

As the Chinese people have united at last;

We dare to take the Yangtze as a long ribbon,

In furious tides we'll show our big ambition;

We dare to hold the Yellow River to the Sky,

In the energetic breeze we'll freely glorify;

We dare to will the sun and the moon freely,

And to call on the wind and cloud willingly;

敢以身为天下先,
一路高歌神州行。
青春之我创青春,
伟大复兴指日等;
厚德包容甘为仆,
万民为重贵虔诚。
为民不怕责任重,
为民不怕始作俑,
为民不怕下炼狱,
为民不怕上九重,
为民敢走不归路,
为民敢把逆鳞撄,
为民洒血书春秋,
为民谱写中国梦!
嫦娥奔月请天命,
吴刚献酒味道浓;
情系芸芸众百姓,
百姓心称最公平。
展望未来明心志,
谨赠一言勉诸公:
改革啊一生一世,
发展啊一世一生;
若道中华国果亡,
除是炎黄俱尽忠。
历经磨难终不悔,
感天动地绘前景;

We dare to behave ourselves as a locomotive,

With high-pitched tune we shall turn active.

We, in time of youth, will act with full vitality,

And our great rebirth will soon run into reality;

With humble virtue we'd like to serve the people,

In loyalty we hold that the people are respectable.

For the people we are not afraid of responsibility,

For the people we are not afraid of trouble makers,

For the people we are not afraid of great tortures,

For the people we are not afraid of big failures,

For the people we dare to go deep into the hell,

For the people we dare to have the truth to tell,

For the people we can dedicate all toward our aim,

For the people we can realize the Chinese Dream!

We are sincere like Chang'e who would not decline,

And we are cordial like Wu Gang who made wine:

Our hearts are tied to the interests of the people,

And their judgment is of most just and valuable.

In face of future we have our ambitions to show,

And there is a word presented for all of you:

For all our life we'll embrace the great reform,

And in all our life we'll meet tests of any form;

Our country will never be perished on earth,

Unless all the Chinese have met their death.

After a sea of hardships we shall never vegret,

With a sincerity we'll go on for development;

滚滚黄河奔东海，
滔滔长江人潮涌；
巨手敢创千秋业，
心高气壮放歌行；
华夏铁肩担日月，
共谋寰宇享大同。
雄鹰展翅巨龙吟，
浴火重生凤和鸣；
待我民族复兴日，
我主沉浮东方红！

The Yellow River is rushing to the East China Sea,

And the tides of Yangtze River are wildly free;

With firm hands we dare create greatest feat,

And in high spirit we'll sing out the noble trait;

We dare to shoulder any tough responsibility,

And dare to try together to create a best society.

Lo! eagles are flying and dragons howling,

And the fire-bearing phoenixes are singing,

Wait till the Chinese nation rises again,

China will be a shining sun over the mountain!

跋

诗言志

刘 磊

  诗言志,是我国古代文学评论家对诗的本质特征的认识,也意为诗是言诗人之志的。《追梦》即表达了作者蔡远方的思想、志向、抱负、爱憎和澎湃的诗人之志。

  中国是诗词大国。远方是一位纯粹的中国文化学者,几十年来,他在中国文化的浸润中养成了纯正的文化品质。如今,他不拘一格,创作了这部传统与现代相契合的,有血有肉、有志向、有思想、有信仰的大诗作。

  《追梦》是远方为讴歌新时代、为中华人民共和国七十年华诞而作的长篇诗作。他自豪于中华五千年的灿烂文化,痛心于中华民族近代百年的血泪和耻辱,激动于"不愿做奴隶的人们"翻身而解放,慨叹于四十年改革开放、民族复兴、盛世年华。他以沸腾热血,穷毕生积累、尽平生所学、耗数年心血、倾一腔真情,从灵魂深处流淌出一曲对中华民族沧桑巨变的浩叹之歌。

  对于这数千行长诗,远方能做到字斟句酌、旁征博引、七言长咏,实为难能可贵。足见远方下足了功夫。

  同道为朋,非以功利相结。知音,诤友,心有灵犀,神交意会,以道相导,不经意间已走进对方心灵深处,相识长短便变得无足轻重。

这正是我与文化学者蔡远方结识后的体味。远方孜孜不倦,日日笔耕,为祖国强盛奋力创作,且与时俱进,从无辍笔。又逢盛世,天耀中华,禁不住又使远方挥毫高歌。

新时代为中华儿女创造了一个宏伟的民族复兴舞台,中华儿女驰骋在这个舞台上,各行业齐冲并进,追梦、筑梦、圆梦。

任何一部文学艺术作品,都应该是一个让读者登临的平台。读者凭借这个平台,能够拓宽视野、开阔胸襟、净化灵魂、提升素养。远方创作的史诗《追梦》,即为中外读者构筑了一个这样的精神平台。登上这个平台,有助于我们不忘过去、珍惜今天、开创未来。

愿我们的文化出版业和文学艺术家多多搭建这样的平台;亦愿远方和同道们运用多种文学艺术形式,为读者潜心构筑这种丰富多彩的精神平台。

长篇史诗,岁月钩沉;莫忘历史,图强奋进;坚持改革,追求真理;国歌一曲,引吭长吟。振兴中华,走向中华民族的伟大复兴。可谓诗者之志。

是为跋。

2019年春

Postscript

Poetry Reveals One's Aspiration

Liu Lei

The poetry can reveal one's aspiration. This was the understanding of the poetic nature by the men of letters in ancient China. It means that the poetry is used to express the aspiration of the poet. Whereas, the poem titled *To Seek the Chinese Dream* is the very expression of the thought, ideal, ambition, love and hatred of Cai Yuanfang the author, as well as his passionate poetic aspiration.

China is a country of poetry. Mr. Cai is a pure scholar of the Chinese culture as, in scores of years, he has cultivated his orthodox cultural quality in the fertility of the Chinese culture. Now, he has the courage to innovate and create this poem, in which, full of sincere emotions, of loft aspirations, of deep thoughts, and of iron beliefs, the tradition and the modernity are perfectly combined.

The poem titled *To Seek the Chinese Dream* was created by Mr. Cai to ode the New Era and for celebration of the seventieth anniversary of foundation of the People's Republic of China. He is proud of the Chinese civilization with five thousand years of splendid culture; he is indignant with the hundred-year painful humiliation of the Chinese race; he feels joyous with the liberation of "the people reluctant to be slaves"; he, with pure cordiality, signs for the forty-year reform and opening up, the revival of the Chinese people, and the booming days of China. He, with boiling passion, life-long exertion, all-round exhaustion, and years of sincere dedication, has finally created a majestic enchantment, which, flowing out of the deep of his heart, is used to ode to the earth-shaking changes of the Chinese people.

It's certainly challengeable to complete such a thousand-line long poem as this with exact wording, delicate quotation, vivid expression. It is quite evident that Mr. Cai has conducted full exertions in composition and revision.

True friends should be comrades regardless of utility. As critical bosom friends with mental sympathy for the truth, we have casually gone deep into each other's hearts regardless of the time span of our friendship long or short. This is the very inspiration occurred to me when I have known Mr. Cai Yuanfang, the cultural scholar. Mr. Cai takes great pains everyday to create his literary works for the prosperity of China so much so that he, with his constant literary creation, has been going forward along with the times. And the flourishing and shining age of China, in turn, inspires Mr. Cai to chant heartily for it with his pen.

China's New Era has seen a grand stage of national rejuvenation created for the Chinese people of all walks of life, who are all out on the stage to seek, create and realize the Chinese Dream.

Each work of literature and art should be a platform for the readers to step on, and by means of the platform, the readers can broaden theirviews and minds, purify their souls and improve their qualities. The long poem titled *To Seek the Chinese Dream* created by Mr. Cai proves to be such a spiritual platform created for the readers at home and abroad, which is helpful for us to keep the past in mind, to cherish today, and to create the future. I wish our cultural publishing industry and literary artists to build more such platforms, and I also wish Mr. Cai, together with his colleagues, to devote himself to building this colorful spiritual platform for the readers in various forms of literature and art.

As the long poem has traced back our old days, we should not forget about our historical humiliations in the heroic march for national prosperity, but hold fast the reform in our pursuit for the truth. At each time when the national anthem is chanted, it should remind us of the great mission that China will be revitalized toward the great revival of the Chinese people! That is the very aspiration of Mr. Cai.

So much for the passage as a postscript.

Spring, 2019

后 记

蔡远方

一、从《复兴之歌》到《中兴之歌》，再到《追梦》的创作过程

2011年10月10日，为纪念辛亥革命100周年，我在报纸上发表了千行史诗《复兴之歌》（原文是三千行）。这些诗其实是我从2005年开始下笔的。后来，相关杂志又全文刊登了我的长诗。当时，我想结集成书出版。我和二月河老师是老朋友，想让他为我的书题序，因此我专程赴南阳，在市政府马成瑞君的陪同下，到二月河老师家喝茶。老师欣然同意，并嘱我，他写好后会交马成瑞君寄我，就不用我再于北京、南阳之间往返了。

茶间，二月河老师说，明年（2012年）党的十八大要召开，国家的改革开放力度会继续加大，建议我再写一部《中兴之歌》。

2012年秋，党的十八大成功召开，习近平同志任党的总书记（次年春，又担任国家主席）。果然，全国又掀起了强劲的深化改革大潮。

习近平总书记在参观"复光之路"展览时提出和阐述了"中国梦"——"实现中华民族的伟大复兴，就是近代以来最伟大的梦想"，又在2013年至2015年提出并完善了"一带一路"的构想。这样一来，格调变了，格局变了。十八大之后，全国上下强劲改革，强力反腐，

飞速发展，日新月异，人心振奋。我决心再写一部《中兴之歌》。

几年间，《之江心语》《习近平用典》《习近平讲故事》《新理念新思想新战略80词》等好书相继出版，我由粗读到精读，对习近平总书记的雄才大略、宏伟蓝图了然于胸。依凭几十年诗词功底，反复二十余稿，终于在党的十九大召开后的2019年之初，将完整的《追梦》完稿。

《追梦》全稿原为五千行诗，从1917年李大钊先生推崇"十月革命"，著书立说，写到2018年党的十九大，中国百余年历史，惊涛骇浪；其中着重写了1949年至2019年中国七十年的风云变幻；重点创作了习近平同志担任党和国家领导人以来祖国的繁荣富强，展望了至21世纪中期祖国的"圆梦"景色。

此书稿最后定名为《追梦》时，西南大学外国语学院的孟凡君教授所负责的《追梦》后三千行诗句的中译英工作刚好"杀青"。定稿之际，我从最初的五千行诗中精选出近三千行，删去了1917年至新中国成立前后的个别章节，以使内容更加精炼。

令我遗憾、伤怀的是，曾指导我创作的周鸿俊老师、金桐老师、二月河老师先后驾鹤西去。手捧着二月河老师的珍贵序言，我百感交集，不能自已。因此，亦以此书呈献给我最敬爱的二月河老师。清明时节，我将用我新出版的诗集告慰老师的在天之灵。

二、感谢

此书稿从2005年创作至今，受到众多师长和朋友们的指导、帮助和支持。他们分别是：

周鸿俊　作家
金　桐　中国戏曲学院教授
二月河　著名作家
艾　平　中共中央对外联络部原副部长
李佩伦　中央民族大学教授
孟继有　北京大学教授
沈卫星　《光明日报》副总编辑
李　杰　《人民日报》河南分社原社长
龚达发　《人民日报》文艺部原主任
陆　翱　北京京剧院原副院长
张维扬　中国戏曲学院教授
俞　杰　中央民族大学戏剧艺术中心教授
王立群　河南大学教授
常之秋　河南工程学院教授
熊　辉　西南大学教授，中国新诗词研究所所长
孟凡君　西南大学外国语学院教授
刘　磊　中原出版传媒集团副总裁
王刘纯　中原出版传媒集团编审
王洪应　河南省文联副主席，河南省文学艺术评论学会会长
何　弘　河南文学院院长
刘景亮　河南省艺术研究院研究员
王超群　《河南日报》郑州分社原社长
苏建平　北京大学光华管理学院管理中心主任

刘光访　郑州市政协民族宗教委员会主任

马成瑞　南阳市人民政府办公室原主任

尤其要感谢的是孟凡君教授。他为使此书能供海内外读者阅读，冒着酷暑，将所有中文译成英文，将中文诗词变成了优美的英语诗歌。愿此书能让全世界的读者领略中国的神奇之梦，以了我和孟君之愿。

我的妻子刘洋，自我创作此书稿始，一直帮我查资料、校史证，常常与我一起彻夜不眠，伏案疾书。"军功章"有妻一半。

爱女依心六岁时，已能为我搬书找典：《诗经》、《离骚》、李白诗集、苏轼诗词集、莎士比亚全集、泰戈尔作品集……识先翁，吃名典。望她能承父衣钵，2050年续写《圆梦》。

还有，此书在创作、出版过程中，承蒙多位师长、朋友关心关爱，在此一并感谢！

鉴于本人学识有限，诗作难免错谬百出，在此，欢迎广大读者、专家、同仁批评指正！

2019年春日，写于北京独书斋

Epilogue

Cai Yuanfang

I. My Literary Creation from *Ode to China's Revival* to *Ode to China's Resurgence*, and to *To Seek the Chinese Dream*

On October 10th, 2011, in memory of the hundredth anniversary of the 1911 Revolution, I had my thousand-line epic titled *Ode to China's Revival* published on newspaper. The original poem, three thousand lines in total, began to be created in 2005 actually. Later, the long poem of mine was again published in some related journals. And after that, I wanted to get the poems published as a book. As Mr. Er Yuehe is one of my old friends, I asked him to write a preface for my book. With this purpose, I went to Nanyang City, and, accompanied by Mr. Ma Chengrui, an official of the government of Nanyang City, paid a visit to Mr. Er Yuehe. The great literary master accepted my requirement cheerfully, and exhorted me that, when the preface was completed, he should let Mr. Ma hand it over to me lest I would cover a long way from Beijing to Nanyang for it.

During my visit, Mr. Er Yuehe told me that The Eighteenth National Congress of CPC would be convened in the next year (2012), and that China's reform and opening up would be intensified deeply, and then he suggested that I should create another epic titled *Ode to China's Resurgence*. Mr. Er Yuehe was one of the representatives of the congress as well as a man of top wisdom, thus his words are for sure something of inspiration.

In the autumn of 2012, the Eighteenth National Congress of CPC was successfully convened, and comrade Xi Jinping was appointed as the general secretary of the Party (he was also appointed as the president of the People's Republic of China in the spring of 2013). Sure enough, all China began to be swept with strong tides of deepened reform.

General Secretary Xi Jinping proposed and elaborated the idea of The Chinese Dream when he visited the ethibition titled *on the Road to Rejuvehation, namely*, "The realization of the great revival of the Chinese people is the greatest dream since modern times." During from 2013 to 2015, he presented and improved the conception of *One Belt and One Road*. Along with this, great changes have taken place in the situations and patterns of China. Since the Eighteenth National Congress of the CPC, great efforts have been exerted to undertake reform forcibly and to fight against corruption severely, so much so that China has taken an amazing and exciting drastic new look. Thus, I was determined to create another epic titled *Ode to China's Resurgence*.

In the following years, various wonderful works such as *Zhijiang Review*, *Classics Quoted by Xi Jinping*, *Tales Told by Xi Jinping*, and *80 Terms on New Ideas, New Thoughts and New Strategies*, etc., have been published one after another. By reading them from initially to intensively,

I've known very well about the high talent, grand strategy and majestic political scheme of General Secretary Xin Jinping. By means of my scores of years of poetic capacity, and with more than twenty revisions, the total work of *To Seek the Chinese Dream* was completed on January 1st, 2019, after the convening of the 19th National Congress of the Communist party of China.

The original poem of *To Seek the Chinese Dream* is composed of five thousand lines, covering the time span from 1917, when Li Dazhao highly praised the October Revolution by writing books and articles, to 2018, when the Nineteenth National Congress of CPC was convened. The hundred years of the Chinese history has witnessed seas of hardships and disasters. Among these, the time span is highlighted from 1949 to 2019, seventy years in total since the foundation of the People's Republic of China with great changes and gradual developments throughout it, with the focuson China's prosperity, strength and other great achievements since the leadership of general secretary Xi Jinping. At last, there in the poem is the prospect for realization of the Chinese Dream in the 2050s.

When the poem was finally titled as *To Seek the Chinese Dream*, Professor Meng Fanjun, who is from College of International Studies, Southwest University, had just finished the transtation of the later part of the poem (three thousand lines in total) into English. Certain chapters or sections related to the period before and after the founding of the People's Republic of China were omitted, and I selected nearly three thousand lines from my five-thousand-line poem so that there is a perfect match between the content and the title.

What is regretful and sorrowful to me is the fact that Mr. Zhou Hongjun, Mr. Jin Tong and Mr. Er Yuehe, who had given me a lot of direction for my poetic creation, passed away one after another. I am overwhelmed with a great variety of passions every time when I palm the precious preface by Mr. Er Yuehe. Thus, I will dedicate the book to Mr. Er Yuehe, my most beloved tutor. And in middle spring of each year, I will comfort with the new edition of this poem Mr. Er Yuehe, who is still alive in heaven.

II. My Thanks

I want to thank all my tutors and friends, who, since my creation of the poem in 2005, have given me a lot of directions, assistances and supports. They are as follows:

Mr. Zhou Hongjun, writer

Mr. Jin Tong, professor of National Academy of Chinese Theatre Arts

Mr. Er Yuehe, distinguished writer

Mr. Ai Ping, former vice minister of International Department. Central Committee of CPC

Mr. Li Peilun, professor of the Minzu University of China

Mr. Meng Jiyou, professor of Peking University

Mr. Shen Weixing, deputy editor-in-chief of *Guangming Daily*

Mr. Li Jie, former director of Henan Branch of *People's daily*

Mr. Gong Dafa, former director of the Division of Literature and Arts of *People's daily*

    Mr. Lu Ao, former president of Jingju Theater Company of Bejing

    Mr. Zhang Weiyang, professor of National Academy of Chinese Theatre Arts

    Ms. Yu Jie, professor of Drama Art Center of the Minzu University of China

    Mr. Wang Liqun, professor of Henan University

    Mr. Chang Zhiqiu, professor of Henan University of Engineering

    Mr. Xiong Hui, professor of Southwest University and dean of Institute of New Poetry

    Mr. Meng Fanjun, professor of College of International Studies, Southwest University

    Mr. Liu Lei, vice president of Central China Publish

    Mr. Wang Liuchun, senior editor of Central China Publish

    Mr. Wang Hongying, vice chairman of Henan Literature and Art Union, director of Henan Society for Literary and Artistic Criticism

    Mr. He Hong, dean of Henan College of Liberal Arts

    Mr. Liu Jingliang, researcher of Henan Academy of Arts

    Mr. Wang Chaoqun, former director of Zhengzhou Branch of *Henan Daily*

    Mr. Su Jianping, Director of management Center, Guanghua School of Management, Peking University

    Mr. Liu Guangfang, Director of Ethnic and Religious Committee of Zhengzhou Municipal People's Political Consultative Conference

    Mr. Ma Chengrui, former Office Director of the People's Government of Nanyang City

Special thanks should be given to Professor Meng Fanjun, who, in order to have the poem read by various readers all over the world, made great efforts to translate it into English. I wish people all over the world would appreciate the wonderful Chinese Dream, and for which the great expectation both of me and of Professor Meng will be realized.

And special thanks should be given to Liu Yang, my wife, who, since my creation of the poem from the very beginning, has been exerting all her efforts to help me check the information and proofread the historical evidences related to my creation. She had constantly worked from dusk to dawn, toiling hard at the desk. Thus she should securely deserve half of my achievements!

Yixin, my dear daughter, who is at the age of six, has been a little assistant of mine by looking for and carrying books, such as Book of Songs, Lisao, Poems by Li Bai, Ci Poems by Su Shi, Complete Works by William Shakespeare and Works by Tagore…Being amazed at her acuteness in reciting the poetic lines or sentences for the classics by the former masters, I am so eager that she, as my successor, could have created another epic titled Realization of the Chinese Dream by 2050 .

Besides, I will give thanks to all those who have taken care of me cordially during my creation and publication of this work!

Some errors or mistakes may be inevitably seen in this work, Isincerely invite readers, experts, colleagues to correct!

Dushu Study, Beijing, in the spring of 2019

致读者

关于《追梦》的几句嘱语

一、因汉语和英语的语法结构、语音感受差别较大，故译者在汉译英时，为使诗句押韵、流畅和完整，在个别句子和细节里，英文追求的是意境相同，而非字词的一一对应。

二、诗者本意是想让国外读者在享受诗歌美感的同时，了解中国文化、中国思想的纵向发展，并与西方文化、西方思想进行横向比较。但是，这部作品毕竟是诗歌，可能无法做到尽如人意，如果国外读者想要深入探究中国历史、感受中国文化的美妙，只能来美丽的东方寻觅了。

三、本书译者是中国西南大学外国语学院教授孟凡君先生。孟先生在繁忙的教学、研究之余潜心作译，真是难能可贵。在此，本人再次致以深深谢忱！

愿国内外读者都能够感受到伟大的中国梦。

蔡远方

2019 年春日，写于北京独书斋

Note to Readers Regarding the Translations of *To Seek the Chinese Dream*

1. Since Chinese is quite different from English in grammatical structures and phonetic features, the translator, when translating the Chinese poem into English, has to adjust certain original sentences and detailed expressions in order to achieve the poetic flavor in rhyme, fluency and integrity with a view to the equivalence artistically rather than literally.

2. The poet's original intention is to let the English readers understand the development of China's culture and thought in comparison with the culture and thought of the west while enjoying the beauty of poetry. But, it is a poem after all, and if the English readers want to delve into the beauty of the Chinese history and culture, they have to go deeper into the Oriental culture.

3. This long poem is translated by Meng Fanjun, professor of College of International Studies, Southwest University, China. It's truly praiseworthy that Mr. Meng has devoted himself to the translation of the poem along with his busy work as a teacher and scholar, for which I hereby would like to express my deep gratitude tohim!

I hope that readers at home and abroad will be charmed by the great Chinese Dream.

Cai Yuanfang
Dushu Study, Beijing, in the spring of 2019